A SHEEP REMEMBERS

David B. Calhoun (1937–2021)

Courtesy of Covenant Theological Seminary

A SHEEP REMEMBERS

David B. Calhoun

'The LORD is my Shepherd.'

Psalm 23:1.

THE BANNER OF TRUTH TRUST

THE BANNER OF TRUTH TRUST

Head Office
3 Murrayfield Road
Edinburgh, EH12 6EL
UK

North America Office
610 Alexander Spring Road
Carlisle, PA 17015
USA

banneroftruth.org

© David B. Calhoun 2021
Reprinted 2023

*

ISBN
Print: 978 1 80040 079 5
EPUD: 978 1 80040 080 1

*

Typeset in 10/13 Minion Pro at
The Banner of Truth Trust, Edinburgh

Printed in the USA by
Versa Press Inc.,
East Peoria, IL.

To Anne
*A beloved sheep
of the Lord's pasture*

CONTENTS

PREFACE

You are holding the last book of a true shepherd who knew what it is to be one of Christ's sheep.

It is a rich, biblical, theological, experiential, devotional meditation on the Twenty-third Psalm, combined with a testimony to God's faithfulness by a godly pastor and professor who is now at home with his Good Shepherd, having long lived in the valley of the shadow of death. David B. Calhoun (1937–2021) was one of the great church historians and historical theologians of our time, but he was also a missionary and a minister. Dr Calhoun was less well-known than he should have been, but he was deeply appreciated and beloved by those who were blessed to know him. He was brilliant, humble, godly, faithful and kind. A true follower of Jesus.

Professor Calhoun was a friend and mentor to me, a father in the faith. He taught Church History at Covenant Theological Seminary for 30 years (1978–2008) and battled cancer the last four decades of his life (1987–2021). The Lord called him home just as this book had been safely delivered into the hands of the good folk of Banner of Truth. I took every course that I could with him in my seminary days: Ancient and Medieval Church History, Reformation and Modern Church History, Calvin's *Institutes*, History of the

Reformed Tradition, Southern Presbyterian History and Theology, and more. We travelled Scotland together (along with his son Allen) while I was studying at Edinburgh.

He was dear to me and good to me. No one in my seminary education had a greater impact upon my life, doctrine or view of the ministry than David. It is not too much to say that I would never have become the Chancellor of Reformed Theological Seminary if not for his investment in me. David was a studious and learned man. In addition to his undergraduate and Bachelor of Divinity degrees, he held two Master of Theology (ThM) degrees, one in Old Testament and the other in New Testament, and his PhD (Princeton) was in Church History/Historical Theology (writing on the history of Princeton Seminary and missions, 1812–1862). He loved the theology and writings of John Calvin, but he was also an expert in the theology of Henry Bullinger, one of the important early Reformers, and he tipped me off to what has become known as the 'Muller thesis' (the continuity of Reformation and Post-Reformation Reformed theology, over against the now discredited 'Calvin *versus* the Calvinists' historiography so popular among twentieth-century Barthians) before I ever read Richard Muller's *Christ and the Decree*. But David never wore his credentials or his learning on his sleeve. He shared his knowledge freely to edify others, but never flaunted his scholarship.

David was born in Kentucky, but he and I considered one another fellow South Carolinians. We shared a love of history and church history. While I was the Minister of First Presbyterian Church in Jackson, Mississippi, I reached out to David to write our church history as we approached our 175th anniversary in 2012. He had written wonderful church histories of First Presbyterian Church, Columbia, South Carolina, Independent Presbyterian Church, Savannah, Georgia, and First Presbyterian Church, Augusta, Georgia, and he was the perfect person to write the story of yet another historic Southern church. At first he agreed, but then another recurrence of cancer and the attendant side effects of his treatment led the doctors to forbid him to undertake the travel necessary to write the book. He sent me a note declining the task with regret, to which he appended the words: 'It would be nice to have only one terminal illness, but, as always, the Lord knows best.' Such was his acceptance of God's providence (a theme that you will surely see in the pages of this book).

David's courses on church history were always richly devotional and filled with wonderful prayers and quotations. Reading this book brings back memories of sitting in the classroom listening to him lecture, and I can hear the words in his voice as I read. I even hear the cadence of his delivery. This is an unusual book, but it is quintessential David Calhoun. It reads a little like Spurgeon's *Treasury of David*, but with a focus just on Psalm 23.

Each chapter contains a rendering or version of the psalm, followed by a commentary peppered with rich quotations, then more prayers, quotations and stories, and concluding with Dr Calhoun's own testimony to God's faithfulness. The simplicity of his testimonies is striking and instructive, and often disguises the profundity of the spiritual help they will give to the attentive reader.

I can see this little volume being used in several different ways. It could be read straight through, like any other book, of course, but it could also be a helpful companion to any preacher or teacher working through an exposition of the Twenty-third Psalm. Again, it could be read devotionally, a section at a time, perhaps a chapter per day, over ten days (since Dr Calhoun considers the psalm in ten parts), but such a devotional use could be extended by a continued daily use of the various versions of Psalm 23 in the addendum. And don't fail to read the notes in the bibliography at the end. You will get a feel for the author's wide reading in the book's citations, and his annotations of books will give you an insight into how best to benefit from them.

One of the books David edited and introduced is *Prayers on the Psalms*.[1] These prayers were composed in French by Huguenot minister and martyr Augustin Marlorat, and then later translated into English and included in the Scottish Psalter of 1595. The prayer for Psalm 23 reads thus:

> Eternal and Everlasting Father, fountain of all felicity, we render thee praise and thanks that thou hast made known to us our Pastor and Defender who will deliver us from the power of our adversaries. Grant unto us that we, casting away all fear and terror of death, may embrace and confess thy truth, which it has pleased thee to reveal to us by thy Son, our Lord and sovereign Master, Christ Jesus. Amen

David Calhoun spent almost half his life walking through the valley of the shadow of death in his long battle

---

[1] *Prayers on the Psalms: From the Scottish Psalter of 1595* (Edinburgh: Banner of Truth Trust, 2010).

with cancer. He has now stepped out of the shadows into the reality. *A Sheep Remembers* renders to the Father praise and thanks, for revealing to him the Son, Christ Jesus, the great Shepherd of the Sheep (Hebrews 13:20), whom he even now sees face to face.

LIGON DUNCAN
Reformed Theological Seminary
April 2021

PSALM 23

King James Version 1611

[1] The LORD is my shepherd; I shall not want.

[2] He maketh me to lie down in green pastures: he leadeth me beside the still waters.

[3] He restoreth my soul: he leadeth me in the paths of righteousness for his name's sake.

[4] Yea, though I walk through the valley of the shadow of death, I will fear no evil: for thou art with me; thy rod and thy staff they comfort me.

[5] Thou preparest a table before me in the presence of mine enemies: thou anointest my head with oil; my cup runneth over.

[6] Surely goodness and mercy shall follow me all the days of my life: and I will dwell in the house of the LORD for ever.

THIS translation of Psalm 23 is from the King James Bible of 1611. The English Standard Version of 2001 follows it almost word for word.

INTRODUCTION

THE Twenty-third Psalm is probably the best known of all the chapters of the Bible and among the most memorable words ever written in any language. Frank Crossley Morgan said that this psalm 'is one of the great-little psalms. Great in a thousand different ways. Little only in its length. And like all truly great things it is simple – sublimely simple and yet simply sublime.'[1] Psalm 23 is for everyone. It appeals to children, who love sheep and especially lambs. They pray,

> Jesus, tender shepherd, hear me,
> bless thy little lambs tonight.

The psalm invites busy and tired women and men to enjoy 'green grass' and to rest beside 'quiet waters in the Shepherd's care.' It sustains the sick and comforts the old.

Psalm 23 is so familiar that we sometimes think that we can learn nothing more from it. Charles Haddon Spurgeon preached on this psalm at least five or six times. He began one of these sermons, 'I cannot say anything new on this text ... but I can remind you of old and precious truths.'[2] Some may think that Psalm 23 is too sentimental, but there

[1] Frank Crossley Morgan, *A Psalm of an Old Shepherd: A Devotional Study of Psalm 23* (London: Marshall, Morgan & Scott, 1946), 19.

[2] C. H. Spurgeon, *Metropolitan Tabernacle Pulpit*, 52:457.

is within it not only 'green grass' and 'quiet waters' but 'the valley of the shadow of death.' Derek Kidner writes: 'Depth and strength underlie the simplicity of this psalm. Its peace is not escape; its contentment is not complacency: there is readiness to face deep darkness and imminent attack.'[3]

Psalm 23 is a psalm 'of David.' Some scholars have questioned the authenticity of the Psalter's superscriptions, but Bruce Waltke argues persuasively that they are accurate and that 'of David' means 'by David.' Waltke states that 'David authored the psalms attributed to him, and that the historical notices that associate fourteen psalms with his career are credible.'[4] From leading his flock of sheep, David was called by God to lead the flock of Israel. God 'chose David his servant and took him from the sheepfolds; from following the nursing ewes he brought him to shepherd Jacob his people, Israel his inheritance' (Psa. 78:70, 71).

F. B. Meyer believed that David must have written Psalm 23 when he could look back on the experiences of his turbulent life and had 'fully tested the shepherd graces of the Lord of whom he sings.'[5] Frank Crossley Morgan wrote that in Psalm 23 David recalled his life as a shepherd, remembering the many things he had done for his sheep, when he in effect said to himself, 'everything I did once for the sheep, God has been doing for me all along the pathway of my life.'[6]

[3] Derek Kidner, *Psalms 1–72* (Downers Grove: InterVarsity, 1973), 109.

[4] Bruce K. Waltke & James M. Houston, *The Psalms as Christian Worship: A Historical Commentary* (Grand Rapids: Eerdmans, 2010), 92.

[5] F. B. Meyer, *The Shepherd Psalm* (New York: Revell, 1895). 18.

[6] Morgan, *A Psalm of an Old Shepherd*, 21.

I have tried to explain the words of Psalm 23 as David meant them, but also in the fuller light of the New Testament, a light that the psalmist partially saw. Psalm 23 is about the Lord Jesus Christ. He is the 'good Shepherd' who gave his life for his sheep (John 10:11). He is the 'great Shepherd' whom God 'brought again from the dead' (Heb. 13:20). He is the 'chief Shepherd' who one day will give 'the unfading crown of glory' to his faithful under-shepherds (1 Pet. 5:4). And wonder of wonders, the Shepherd became the Lamb who by his sacrificial death 'takes away the sin of the world' (John 1:29). When the great multitude from every nation gather in heaven, 'the Lamb will be their shepherd, and he will guide them to springs of living water' (Rev. 7:17).

Thinking about Psalm 23, we will consider first what the shepherd does for his sheep. Then we will see how this illustrates what God does for 'his people ... the sheep of his pasture' (Psa. 100:3). Leslie Weatherhead's study of Psalm 23 is titled *A Shepherd Remembers*. I call my book *A Sheep Remembers*. With David, 'I remember the days of old; I meditate on all that you have done; I ponder the work of your hands" (Psa. 143:5).

For each chapter of *A Sheep Remembers* I have selected a version of the Twenty-third Psalm or a hymn that is based on the psalm. The chapters of the book are divided into four parts: commentary on the verse or part of the verse that is treated in that chapter; writings from shepherds that help us to understand sheep and their ways; prayers, quotations, and stories illustrating the theme of the chapter; and, in the last place, my own testimony.

Frank Crossley Morgan's book is called *A Psalm of an Old Shepherd*. My book is a 'testimony from an old Christian,' reaching back over seventy-five years to when I was a five-year-old boy. I know that my memory is selective and faulty, but I have tried to be honest and truthful in telling my story, in the presence of the Lord who 'searches the heart and tests the mind' (Jer. 16:9, 10). My life has been far from perfect because of my sin, but it has been a good life, indeed a wonderful life, because of the faithfulness of my Shepherd. In writing my testimony I have tried to keep in mind some wise words from *Finishing Well to the Glory of God* by John Dunlop, a contemporary Christian physician: 'If we have reflected on the good and bad of our lives, now [as we approach the end] is the time to share some of what we will leave behind. One way to do this is by writing what I call "an autobiography of grace." Write your life story with God as the main character, not you.'[7]

> May I never profess more than I actually experience, but may the hidden things of my heart be richer and fuller and deeper than I express to any but you, O Searcher of hearts.[8]

[7] John Dunlop, *Finishing Well to the Glory of God: Strategies from a Christian Physician* (Wheaton: Crossway, 2011), 113.

[8] *Daily Prayers of F. B. Meyer* (Fearn: Christian Focus, 2007). Prayer for January 24.

ONE

THE LORD IS MY SHEPHERD.

Scottish Psalter

1650

The LORD's my Shepherd, I'll not want;
  He makes me down to lie
In pastures green; he leadeth me
  The quiet waters by.

My soul he doth restore again;
  And me to walk doth make
Within the paths of righteousness,
  E'en for his own name's sake.

Yea, though I walk in death's dark vale,
  Yet will I fear none ill,
For thou art with me; And thy rod
  And staff me comfort still.

My table thou hast furnishèd
  In presence of my foes;
My head thou dost with oil anoint,
  And my cup overflows.

> Goodness and mercy all my life
> > Shall surely follow me:
> And in God's house for evermore
> > My dwelling place shall be.

SCOTTISH Christians sang metrical versions of the Psalms, translated into English from Luther's German, as early as the 1540s. In 1556 English exiles in Geneva published a book of fifty-one metrical psalms, and in 1564 the complete Psalter, known as the St Andrews Psalter, was issued. A revision of this Psalter was produced by the Westminster Assembly in 1650 and is still in use.

COMMENTARY

The LORD is my shepherd

Martin Luther said that the words 'The Lord is my shepherd' are 'brief but also very impressive and apt. The world glories and trusts in honour, power, riches, and the favour of men. Our psalm, however, glories in none of these, for they are all uncertain and perishable. "The Lord is my shepherd" speaks a sure, certain faith, which turns its back on everything temporal and transitory, however noble and precious it may be, and turns its face and heart directly to the Lord, who alone is Lord and is and does everything.' 'In this single little word "shepherd,"' Luther said, 'there are gathered together in one almost all the good and comforting things that we praise in God.'[1]

Every word of the first sentence of Psalm 23 is important.

---

[1] *Luther's Works*, vol. 12 (St Louis: Concordia, 1955), 157, 152.

The Lord *is my shepherd*

The psalm does not say that 'God is my shepherd.' It says 'the LORD is my shepherd.' 'God' reflects his eternity and power – 'In the beginning, God created the heavens and the earth' (Gen. 1:1). 'LORD' suggests his love and care – 'For you, O LORD, are good and forgiving, abounding in steadfast love to all who call upon you' (Psa. 86:5). 'LORD' is God's personal name. In the Hebrew Old Testament it is YHWH or 'Yahweh.' This is rendered 'LORD' (in small capital letters) in the English Standard Version, and most modern translations, although in some it appears as 'Jehovah.'

In the Old Testament one's name represented a person's innermost nature and character. In Exodus 3:13-15, Moses said to God,

> 'If I come to the people of Israel and say to them, "The God of your fathers has sent me to you," and they ask me, "What is his name?" what shall I say to them?' God said to Moses, 'I AM WHO I AM.' And he said, 'Say this to the people of Israel, "I AM has sent me to you."' God also said to Moses, 'Say this to the people of Israel, "The LORD, the God of your fathers, the God of Abraham, the God of Isaac, and the God of Jacob, has sent me to you." This is my name forever, and thus I am to be remembered throughout all generations.'

In Exodus 6:3-8, God repeated his covenant-name 'LORD' and promised to act in a decisive way on behalf of his people – 'I will bring you out,' 'I will deliver you,' 'I will redeem you,' 'I will take you to be my people,' 'I will be your God,' 'I will bring you into the land,' and 'I will give it to you for a possession.' 'I AM WHO I AM' is translated by Bernard

Childs 'I will be who I will be' – pointing to God's ongoing future action for his people.[2]

F. Crossley Morgan suggests that God's promise in Exodus 3 and 6 'is somewhat analogous to that of a blank cheque. It is as though God said, "I am – whatever my people need."'[3] Our first and greatest need is to be saved from our sins. Charles Haddon Spurgeon said that Psalm 22 is 'the Psalm of the Cross,' and added, 'It is only after we have read, "My God, my God, why hast thou forsaken me?" that we come to "The Lord is my shepherd."'[4] Robert Murray M'Cheyne preached that Christ was forsaken by the Father as he bore in his own body the sins of the world. 'If you close with him, as your surety,' M'Cheyne said, 'you will never be forsaken. Jesus cried, "My God, why hast thou forsaken me?" I can answer, for me – for me! It was for me that he was forsaken by the Father.'[5]

> Lo, the Good Shepherd for the sheep is offered;
> The slave hath sinned, and the Son hath suffered;
> > For our atonement,
> > While we nothing heeded,
> > > God intercedeth.
>
> > > > (Johann Heerman, 1585–1647)

In her *Crosswicks Journals* Madeleine L'Engle writes that one night her four-year-old son ended his bedtime prayer,

[2] Quoted in J. Todd Billings, *Rejoicing in Lament: Wrestling with Incurable Cancer & Life in Christ* (Grand Rapids: Brazos Press, 2015), 48.

[3] Morgan, *A Psalm of an Old Shepherd*, 32.

[4] C. H. Spurgeon, *The Treasury of David*, third edition (New York: Funk & Wagnalls, 1885), 398.

[5] R. M. M'Cheyne, *Sermons* (London: Banner of Truth Trust, 1961), 47-49.

'And, God, remember to be the Lord.' The psalmists hold before God his covenant name and his covenant promises, as in Psalm 25:6: 'Remember your mercy, O LORD, and your steadfast love, for they have been from of old'; and Psalm 74:18, 20 – 'O LORD … have regard for the covenant.' God, remember to be the LORD.

The LORD is *my shepherd*

David does not pray that the Lord will be his shepherd, but he confidently and joyfully affirms that the Lord *is* his shepherd. There is no 'if' or 'but' or 'I hope so' about it. Psalm 23 is not instruction in the law of the Lord. It is not exhortation. From its first word to its last, it is a testimony of the Lord's love and faithfulness to his people. Dietrich Bonhoeffer told his students that 'we should never forget that every word of Holy Scripture [is] a quite personal message of God's love for us.'[6] That should fill us with joy. 'The most valuable thing the Psalms do for me,' wrote C. S. Lewis, 'is to express the same delight in God which made David dance.'[7]

The LORD *is* my *shepherd*

The Bible says that the Lord is the shepherd of many sheep. 'Then he led forth his people like sheep and guided them in the wilderness like a flock' (Psa. 78:52). 'Give ear, O Shepherd of Israel, you who lead Joseph like a flock' (Psa. 80:1). 'For he is our God and we are the people of his pasture,

[6] Dietrich Bonhoeffer, *My Soul Finds Rest: Reflections on the Psalms* (Grand Rapids: Zondervan, 2002), 34.

[7] C. S. Lewis, *Reflections on the Psalms* (London: Geoffrey P. Bles, 1958), 43.

the flock under his care' (Psa. 95:7). David himself wrote in the last verse of Psalm 28, 'Oh, save your people and bless your heritage! Be their shepherd and carry them forever.' And in one of the most beautiful verses in the Bible we read, 'He will tend his flock like a shepherd; he will gather the lambs in his arms; he will carry them in his bosom, and gently lead those that are with young' (Isa. 40:11). F. B. Meyer writes, 'It is good to know that, in whatever country we are found, under whatever sky, we are, through faith in the divine Saviour, members in the same body, sheep in the same flock, children of the one home.'[8]

The Lord, who is the shepherd of many sheep, is my shepherd. Augustine prayed to God in his *Confessions*, 'You are good and all-powerful, caring for each one of us as though the only one in your care, and yet for all as for each individual.'[9] William Plumer wrote that 'the faith which can truly say, My Shepherd! My Lord! My God! My Rock! turns prophecies into history, promises into deliverances, sorrows into joys, prisons into palaces, perils into victories, death into life.'[10]

J. Sherrard Rice was pastor of First Presbyterian Church in Columbia, South Carolina, from 1959 to 1966. Preaching on Psalm 23, he told the following story:

> A man on his sick bed once confessed to his minister that, although he loved the Psalm, he did not have any personal assurance that it applied to him. The minister

[8] Meyer, *The Shepherd Psalm*, 5.

[9] Augustine, *Confessions*, 3.11.

[10] William S. Plumer, *Psalms: A Critical and Expository Commentary with Doctrinal and Practical Remarks* (Edinburgh: Banner of Truth Trust, 1975), 316-17.

told him to stretch out the five fingers of his left hand, and to count on them the first five words of the Psalm. 'Now,' he said, 'hold tightly on to the fourth finger of your left hand. The Lord is my shepherd! When you can say that, the promises are all your own.' A short time later the man died. When the minister called at the home, the daughter said, 'Father died with a smile of childlike peace; and we noticed that he was holding tightly in his right hand, the fourth finger of his left.' As he met death face to face, he was saying to himself with quiet trust, 'The LORD is my shepherd.'[11]

The LORD is my shepherd

Sheep and shepherds are mentioned in fully half of the books of the Bible. Abel, Abraham, Isaac, Jacob, Rachel, Moses, David, Amos were all shepherds. David was not the first to call the Lord 'my shepherd.' When he was dying, Jacob blessed Joseph's sons Ephraim and Manasseh, saying, 'The God before whom my fathers Abraham and Isaac walked, the God who has been my shepherd all my life long to this day, the angel who has redeemed me from all evil, bless the boys' (Gen. 48:15, 16).

SHEEP AND SHEPHERDS

Margaret Brown managed a sheep farm in Colorado for forty-seven years. Sometimes an itinerant 'sheepherder' named Rube showed up to help her. He came especially, it seemed, in times of crisis. Once on a bitterly cold day

[11] David B. Calhoun, *The Glory of the Lord Risen Upon It: First Presbyterian Church, Columbia, South Carolina, 1795–1995* (Columbia: R. L. Bryan, 1994), 270.

Margaret's ewes started to lamb. She had not prepared a warm place for them. Rube appeared and, hastily gathering firewood, soon had a bonfire roaring. Margaret Brown wrote:

> Then he made another fire a few yards from the first. I realized his plan: the area between the two fires would be relatively warm, and newborn lambs would have a fair chance there. It took a vast amount of wood to keep the great fires going but the result was heartening. We were still at this task when a thin wail came from where the ewes were bedded. I was almost overcome with panic but Rube worked quietly into the bunch and came out a few minutes later carrying a little lamb, the mother following. He deposited the lamb gently near one of the fires.
>
> A yearling lambed next, and Rube carried the newborn even more tenderly. It was scarcely breathing and Rube said we must get this one and its frightened mother into the cabin. 'He came just ahead of schedule, but he'll make it now,' Rube said. He gathered wood, kept the fires roaring, watched the ewes. It was a memorable scene: the soaring flames of the great fires whipped by the furious wind, and the patriarchal old man gently carrying the little lambs.
>
> About midnight, as I went to the cabin to make coffee, I noticed that Rube seemed to be hunting for something near one of the fires, but when I returned he had gone over to the ewes again. Looking down I saw a glint of red. It was a pocket edition of the New Testament and Psalms bound in worn red morocco. By the firelight I could see that many passages had been marked.

Rube came back as I stood holding the little book in my hand. 'I thought I'd lost it,' he said. 'I've had it a long time. It's brought me a long ways.'

'It will take anyone a long way,' I said humbly.

As is the way with mountain blizzards in spring, the storm was spent by dawn. Not a lamb had been lost, and with the hush that follows a storm, peace settled over the camp: the expanse of gray-green sagebrush etched with snow, the quiet sheep, the wild-sweet fragrance of wood smoke from dying fires. As Rube and I sat on the cabin steps drinking coffee I thought again of the little Testament.

'What's your favourite Bible verse, Rube?' I asked.

He answered without hesitation: 'Come unto me, all ye that labour and are heavy laden, and I will give you rest.'

I felt a lump in my throat. Rube asked, 'What's yourn?'

'The first line of the Twenty-third Psalm,' I answered.

'The LORD is my shepherd,' he said softly. 'The one about the sheep.'[12]

* * *

In his classic book about the Holy Land, William Thomson wrote:

Come down to the river. There is something going forward worth seeing. Yon shepherd is about to lead his flock across; and – as our Lord says of the good shepherd – you observe that he goes before, and the sheep follow. Not all in the same manner, however.

[12] Margaret Dawson Brown, *Shepherdess of Elk River Valley*, (Golden Bell Press, 1982).

Some enter boldly and come straight across. These are the loved ones of the flock, who keep hard by the footsteps of the shepherd, whether sauntering through green meadows by the still waters, feeding upon the mountains, or resting at noon beneath the shadow of great rocks. And now others enter, but in doubt and alarm. Far from their guide, they miss the ford, and are carried down the river, some more, some less; and yet, one by one, they all struggle over and make good their landing. Notice those little lambs. They refuse to enter, and must be driven into the stream by the shepherd's dog … Poor things! How they leap and plunge, and bleat in terror! That weak one yonder will be swept quite away, and perish in the sea. But no; the shepherd himself leaps into the stream, lifts the lamb into his bosom, and bears it trembling to the shore. All safely over, how happy they appear! The lambs frisk and gambol about in high spirits, while the older ones gather round their faithful guide, and look up to him in subdued but expressive thankfulness.

Now, can you watch such a scene and not think of that Shepherd who leadeth Joseph like a flock; and of another river, which all his sheep must cross? He, too, goes before, and, as in the case of this flock, they who keep near him fear no evil. They hear his sweet voice saying, 'When thou passeth through the waters, I will be with thee; and through the floods, they shall not overflow thee' (Isa. 43:3). With eye fastened on him, they scarcely see the stream, or feel its cold and threatening waves. The great majority, however, 'linger, shivering on the brink, and fear to launch away.' They lag behind, look down upon the dark river, and, like Peter on stormy Gennesaret, when faith failed, they begin to sink. Then they cry for help, and not in vain. The good Shepherd hastens to their rescue; and none of all his flock can ever perish. Even the weakest lambkins are carried safely over.[13]

PRAYERS, QUOTATIONS, AND STORIES

> Know that the LORD, he is God!
>   It is he who made us,
>   And we are his;
>   We are his people,
>   And the sheep of his pasture.
>
> (Psa. 100:3)

* * *

As one looking into some priceless gem may see fountains of colour welling upward from its depths, so, as we shall gaze into these verses [of Psalm 23], simple as childhood's rhymes, but deep as an archangel's anthem, we shall see in them the gospel in miniature, the grace of God reflected as the sun in a dewdrop, and things which eye hath not seen, nor ear heard, nor the heart of man conceived.[14]

* * *

In one magnificent sentence, Kenneth Bailey tells how the Lord, our Shepherd, provides all that we need – 'food,

[13] W. M. Thomson, *The Land and the Book or Biblical Illustrations Drawn from the Manners and Customs, the Scenes and Scenery of the Holy Land* (London: Thomas Nelson, 1894), 62-63.

[14] Meyer, *The Shepherd Psalm*, 13.

drink, tranquillity, rescue when lost, freedom from fear of evil and death, a sense of being surrounded by the grace of the Lord, and a permanent dwelling place in the house of God.'[15]

* * *

David, though he lived long, never wrote but one twenty-third Psalm. Some of his odes do indeed express as lively a faith as this, and faith can walk in darkness. But where else do we find a whole Psalm expressive of personal confidence, joy and triumph from beginning to end?[16]

* * *

In Bunyan's *Pilgrim's Progress* we read:

Now supper was ready, the table spread, and all things set on the board: so they sat down and did eat, when one had given thanks. And the Interpreter did usually entertain those that lodged with him with music at meals; so the minstrels played. There was also one that did sing, and a very fine voice he had. His song was this:

> The Lord is only my support,
> And he that doth me feed;
> How can I then want any thing
> Whereof I stand in need.

[15] Kenneth E. Bailey, *The Good Shepherd: A Thousand Year Journey from Psalm 23 to the New Testament* (Downers Grove: IVP Academic, 2014), 39.
[16] Plumer, *Psalms*, 317.

My Testimony

My father was a preacher. To illustrate his sermons, my mother sometimes drew chalk pictures on a large easel while the congregation watched and someone played an old upright piano. One Sunday night, in the little church in the pine woods of South Carolina, she drew a picture of a shepherd reaching for a little lamb that had fallen into a crevice on the side of a mountain. The shepherd was leaning far down to rescue the lamb with his staff. The congregation sang 'The Ninety and Nine,' and my father preached about Jesus, the good shepherd.

The song 'The Ninety and Nine' was composed by Ira Sankey, D. L. Moody's song leader. In Scotland, Sankey read a poem written by Elizabeth Clephane, based on Jesus' parable of the lost sheep in Luke 15. Sankey scribbled the poem on a piece of paper and put it in his pocket, and a few days later in Edinburgh, Moody preached on 'The Good Shepherd.' He ended his sermon, turned to Sankey, and asked if he had an appropriate song to sing. Sankey thought of the poem, 'The Ninety and Nine.' He placed the words on the organ in front of him and began to sing. 'Note by note,' he later wrote, 'the tune was given, which has not been changed from that day to this.'

> There were ninety and nine that safely lay
> In the shelter of the fold;
> But one was out on the hills away,
> Far off from the gates of gold.
> Away on the mountains wild and bare;
> Away from the tender Shepherd's care.

Lord, thou hast here thy ninety and nine;
    Are they not enough for thee?
But the Shepherd made answer:
    This of mine has wandered away from me.
And although the road be rough and steep,
    I go to the desert to find my sheep.

But none of the ransomed ever knew
    How deep were the waters crossed;
 Nor how dark was the night the Lord passed
    through
    Ere he found his sheep that was lost,
Out in the desert he heard its cry;
    'Twas sick and helpless and ready to die.

And all through the mountains, thunder-riv'n,
    And up from the rocky steep,
There arose a glad cry to the gate of heav'n,
    Rejoice! I have found my sheep!
And the angels echoed around the throne,
    Rejoice, for the Lord brings back his own.

'Lord, whence are those blood-drops all the way
    That mark out the mountain's track?'
'They were shed for one who had gone astray
    Ere the Shepherd could bring him back.'
'Lord, whence are thy hands so rent and torn?'
    'They're pierced tonight by many a thorn.'

After seeing my mother's picture and hearing my father preach on the Good Shepherd, I said to Mother that night, 'I want Jesus to find me.' She replied, with biblical wisdom I did not understand until much later, 'He already has.'

I sought the Lord, and afterward I knew
   He moved my soul to seek him, seeking me;
It was not I that found, O Saviour true,
   No, I was found of thee.

(Anonymous)

TWO

I SHALL NOT WANT. HE MAKES ME LIE DOWN IN GREEN PASTURES. HE LEADS ME BESIDE STILL WATERS.

JAMES MONTGOMERY

1825

The Lord is my Shepherd, no want shall I know;
    I feed in green pastures, safe folded I rest;
He leadeth my soul where the still waters flow,
    Restores me when wand'ring, redeems when
        oppressed.

Through the valley and shadow of death though I stray,
    Since thou art my guardian, no evil I fear;
Thy rod shall defend me, thy staff be my stay;
    No harm can befall, with my Comforter near.

In the midst of affliction my table is spread;
    With blessings unmeasured my cup runneth o'er;
With perfume and oil thou anointest my head;
    Oh, what shall I ask of thy providence more?

Let goodness and mercy, my bountiful God,
   Still follow my steps till I meet thee above;
I seek, by the path which my ancestors trod,
   Through the land of their sojourn, thy kingdom
     of love.

SCOTTISH by birth and educated in Ireland, James Montgomery became a journalist in England. His father was a Moravian pastor, but James turned his back on the Christian faith. Slowly, he was brought back, sin-burdened and miserable, to the Saviour he had spurned. This hymn is his testimony, with a reference to his Moravian ancestors.

COMMENTARY

He makes me lie down in green pastures. He leads me beside still waters

'No image could have been devised more beautifully descriptive of rest and safety and trustful happiness than that of the sheep lying down in the deep, rich meadow grass, beside the living stream, under the care of a tender and watchful shepherd.'[1] George Lamsa, who grew up in a community of semi-nomadic sheep herders in Syria, describes how God does for us what a shepherd does for his sheep: 'The same shepherd who takes care of the sheep today will look after them tomorrow. When one pasture gives out, another is found and when one well is dried, another is opened. How much more then will God, who is

[1] Stewart Perowne, *The Book of Psalms*, vol. 1 (1864; repr. Grand Rapids: Zondervan, 1966), 248.

unchangeable, and whose love is abundant, look after his people and see that their needs are met every day.'[2]

Sheep need food, water, and rest. So do we, but we need much more. Our lives are filled with wants and longings. Elizabeth Goudge describes one of the characters in her book *Towers in the Mist*: 'The life she wanted seemed always to elude her, to be around her and in front of her and above her, but never quite within her reach. She did not quite know what it was that she wanted, she only knew that it was not what she had.'[3]

The person who does not have the Lord as his or her shepherd, wrote William Plumer, 'may seek and obtain everything catalogued by the wise of earth, and is still a poor creature.'[4] Sooner or later worldly people discover that they "have hewed out cisterns for themselves, broken cisterns that can hold no water" (Jer. 2:13). Augustine wrote in the *Confessions*: 'Where are you going? … What goal are you making for, wandering around and about by ways so hard and laborious? Rest is not where you seek it. Seek what you seek, but it is not where you seek it. You seek happiness of life in the land of death, and it is not there.' It is impossible to find 'happiness of life' – and purpose and meaning except in one place – that is, in one person. Augustine wrote, 'You have made us for yourself, and our heart is restless until it rests in you.'[5]

[2] George Lamsa, *The Shepherd of All: The Twenty-third Psalm* (CreateSpace Independent Publishing Platform, 2014), 47.

[3] Elizabeth Goudge, *The Cathedral Trilogy* (London: Coronet Books, 1986), Book 2, 37.

[4] Plumer, *Psalms*, 317.

[5] Augustine, *Confessions*, 4.12; 1.1.

We need living water. We need the bread of life. We need rest for our souls. Jesus told the Samaritan woman, 'Everyone who drinks of this water will be thirsty again, but whoever drinks of the water that I will give him will never be thirsty forever' (John 4:13, 14). He told a great crowd of people by the Sea of Galilee, whose physical hunger he had met, 'I am the bread of life; whoever comes to me shall not hunger' (John 6:35). He invited the weary, 'Come to me, all who labour and are heavy laden, and I will give you rest' (Matt. 11:28).

I shall not want

Does this mean that I will never want anything? Matthew Henry answers: 'I shall not want [or lack] anything that is really necessary and good for me … I shall be supplied with whatever I need and, if I have not everything I desire, I may conclude it is either not fit for me or not good for me or I shall have it in due time.'[6] John Newton wrote, 'All shall work together for good; everything is needful that he sends; nothing can be needful that he withholds.'[7] These words from Newton, says Timothy Keller, put 'an ocean of biblical theology into a thimble.'[8]

I have made several trips to Haiti for ministry in that country. I travelled from Port-au-Prince to Aux Cayes near the end of the southern peninsula, where I was blessed by

[6] Matthew Henry, *Commentary* (Grand Rapids: Hendrickson, 1991), 3:258.

[7] *Select Letters of John Newton* (Edinburgh: Banner of Truth Trust, 2011), 211.

[8] Timothy Keller, *Walking with God through Pain and Suffering* (New York: Riverhead Books, 2013), 267.

wonderful Christian people. One day a pastor invited me to his home for a meal. His house was little more than a wooden shed. The food was plain, rice and some kind of canned meat. The pastor's wife and children were dressed in their best, but their best was worn and ill fitting. The Haitian pastor gave thanks, 'Lord you are so good to us. You have given us so much.'

According to Matthew Henry, 'The greatest abundance is but a dry pasture to a wicked man, who relishes only in it that which pleases the senses; but to a godly man, who tastes the goodness of God in all his enjoyments, and by faith relishes that, though he has but little of the world, it is a green pasture.'[9] Alexander Maclaren says that 'it is not mainly of outward blessings that the Psalmist was thinking,' when he wrote, 'I shall not want.' Those outward blessings

> are precious chiefly as emblems of the better spiritual gifts; and it is not an accommodation of his words, but is the appreciation of their truest spirit, when we look upon them, as the instinct of devout hearts has ever done, as expressing both God's gifts of temporal mercies, and His gift of spiritual good, of which higher gift all the lower are meant to be significant and symbolic. Thus regarded, the image describes the sweet rest of the soul in communion with God, in whom alone the hungry heart finds food that satisfies, and from whom alone the thirsty soul drinks deep draughts.[10]

[9] Henry, *Commentary*, 3:258.

[10] Alexander Maclaren, Alexander MacLaren, *Expositions of Holy Scripture: The Psalms, Volume 1: Psalms I–XLIX* (London: Hodder & Stoughton, 1892), 97-98.

Sheep and Shepherds

William Thomson wrote:

Our Saviour says that the good shepherd, when he putteth forth his own sheep, goeth before them, and they follow (John 10:4). They are so tame and so trained that they follow their keeper with the utmost docility. He leads them forth from the fold, or from their houses in the village, just where he pleases. As there are many flocks in such a place as this, each [shepherd] takes a different path, and it is his business to find pasture for them. It is necessary, therefore, that they should be taught to follow, and not to stray away in the unfenced fields of corn which lie so temptingly on either side. Any one that thus wanders is sure to get into trouble. The shepherd calls sharply from time to time, to remind them of his presence. They know his voice, and follow on; but, if a stranger call, they stop short, lift up their heads in alarm, and, if the call is repeated, they turn and flee. This is not the fanciful costume of a parable; it is simple fact.

Isaiah has a beautiful reference to the good shepherd: 'He shall feed his flock like a shepherd; he shall gather the lambs with his arm, and carry them in his bosom, and shall gently lead those that are with young' (Isa. 40:11) ... In ordinary circumstances the shepherd does not feed his flock, except by leading and guiding them where they may gather for themselves; but there are times when it is otherwise. Late in autumn, when the pastures are dried up, and in winter, in places covered with snow, he must furnish them food or they die. In the vast oak woods along the eastern sides of Lebanon, between Baalbek and the cedars, there are gathered innumerable flocks, and the shepherds are all day in the bushy trees, cutting down the branches upon whose green leaves and tender twigs the sheep and goats are entirely supported.

Did you ever see a shepherd gather the lambs in his arms, and carry them in his bosom? He will gently lead along the mothers, in those times when to overdrive them even for a single day would cause their death, as Jacob said to his brother [Esau] … 'My lord knoweth that the flocks and herds with young are with me, and if men should overdrive them one day, all the flock would die' (Gen. 33:13).[11]

* * *

Jesus said, 'When [the shepherd of the sheep] has brought out all his own, he goes before them, and the sheep follow him, for they know his voice. A stranger they will not follow, but they will flee from him, for they do not know the voice of strangers' (John 10:4, 5). When Stephen Haboush was given the task of caring for his father's sheep in Galilee, his uncle told him: 'My boy, when you take care of your father's flock, remember to give a certain call and continue to give this call throughout your [life as a shepherd], so that when the sheep hear you they will know your voice and follow you wherever you lead them, for the sheep know not the shepherd by his face and garments, but by his call.'[12] Haboush described how the shepherds would create pools of 'still water' for the sheep:

[11] Thomson, *The Land and the Book*, 202-5.

[12] Stephen A. Haboush, *My Shepherd Life in Galilee with the Exegesis of the Twenty-third Psalm* (New York: Harper and Brothers, 1927; reprinted by the author, 1949), 27.

Shepherds used to come together, whereupon one of them would be selected to stand guard with the flocks on the hillside while the rest of us would go down to the river. Here, with picks, shovels, and spades, we would dig from the river into the pasture ground a trench several rods long, several feet wide, and a few inches deep. When that was completed, we would let the water from the river back up into the ditch, and as it backed up it would become 'still.' Then the shepherds would call their sheep to the still waters there amid green pastures. However, the word 'still' does not mean stagnant. Though the waters are still, they are continually fresh because of the stream which, slowly flowing in and out, causes the water to be calm and clean, so that the sheep may quench their thirst therefrom in safety.[13]

Prayers, Quotations, and Stories

He will supply every need of yours according to his riches in glory in Christ Jesus.

(Phil. 4:19)

* * *

A Morning Prayer from *The Valley of Vision*:[14]

O ever watchful Shepherd,
Lead, guide, tend me this day.

* * *

[13] Haboush, *My Shepherd Life in Galilee*, 61.
[14] 'Morning,' Arthur Bennett, *The Valley of Vision* (Edinburgh: Banner of Truth Trust, 1975).

Commenting on Psalm 9:18, Spurgeon wrote:

The godly poor have great expectations. They expect the Lord to provide them all things necessary for this life and godliness; they expect to see all things working for their good; they expect to have all the closer fellowship with their Lord, who had not where to lay his head; they expect his Second Advent, and to share its glory ... The poor saint singeth many a song which the rich sinner cannot understand.[15]

* * *

Fulfil now, O Lord, the desires and petitions of thy servants, as may be most expedient for them; granting us in this world knowledge of thy truth, and in the world to come life everlasting.[16]

* * *

Martin Luther wrote:

[The prophet David] was not always happy, nor was he at all times able to sing 'The LORD is my Shepherd, I shall not want.' At times he wanted much, almost too much. He would feel neither justice nor God's comfort and help, but only sin, God's wrath, terror, doubt, and the fear of hell, as he laments in many psalms. Nevertheless, he abandons his feelings and holds God to his promise of a coming Messiah and thinks: 'Be it with me as it may. This is still the comfort of my heart, that

[15] C. H. Spurgeon, 'January 15,' *The Cheque Book of the Bank of Faith* (Fearn, Ross-shire: Christian Focus, 1996).

[16] 'A Prayer of St. Chrysostom' concludes the Order of Morning Prayer in the *Book of Common Prayer* (Greenwich, CT: The Seabury Press, 1953), 20.

I have a gracious, merciful Lord, who is my Shepherd, whose word and promise strengthen and comfort me. Therefore, I shall not want.'[17]

My Testimony

Over my bed is a picture I saw in an elevator at St Luke's Hospital in St Louis as I was coming for my regular chemo-therapy treatment. I stopped by the hospital chaplain's office and asked about the print. Would I be able to buy a copy? It was no longer available, the chaplain said, but she would give me the one in the elevator. I took it home and framed it to hang over my bed. At the top are the words, 'The Lord is my shepherd, I shall not want.' Under those words there is the picture of a path with rows of tall trees on each side. Among the trees it is very dark, but at the end of the path there is light. A shepherd is leading his sheep along the dark path toward the light. At the bottom of the print are the words 'St Luke's Hospital,' and, in smaller letters, 'our specialty is you.'

F. B. Meyer says, 'Your life is wonderfully interesting to Him; every step of it is the subject of His thought.'[18] It doesn't matter how ordinary your life seems to you, or how boring it is. It doesn't matter how young you are or how old. It doesn't matter whether you are in good or ill health. It doesn't matter whether you are rich or poor. It doesn't matter whether you are black or white or any other colour. The Lord finds you wonderfully interesting because you

[17] *Luther's Works*, 12:159.
[18] Meyer, *The Shepherd Psalm*, 69.

are you. He made you just as you are. He is thinking about you and planning for you every day of your life. You are his specialty. 'Know that the LORD, he is God! It is he who made us, and we are his; we are his people, and the sheep of his pasture' (Psa. 100:3).

THREE

HE RESTORES MY SOUL.

HORATIUS BONAR

1843

I was a wandering sheep,
   I did not love the fold;
I did not love my Shepherd's voice,
   I could not be controlled.
I was a wayward child,
   I did not love my home;
I did not love my Father's voice,
   I loved afar to roam.

The Shepherd sought his sheep,
   The Father sought his child;
They followed me o'er vale and hill,
   O'er deserts waste and wild:
They found me nigh to death,
   Famished and faint and lone;
They bound me with the bands of love,
   They saved the wand'ring one.

> Jesus my Shepherd is;
>   'Twas he that loved my soul,
> 'Twas he that washed me in his blood,
>   'Twas he that made me whole;
> 'Twas he that sought the lost,
>   That found the wand'ring sheep,
> 'Twas he that brought me to the fold,
>   'Tis he that still does keep.

HORATIUS BONAR, who descended from a long line
of Presbyterian ministers, was a Free Church of Scotland preacher. Simplicity and devotional warmth mark
his hymns. In Book 3 of the *Confessions* St Augustine
described his own rebellious youth in words similar to
Bonar's hymn: he was, he said, 'an unhappy sheep wandering from [God's] flock.'

COMMENTARY

He restores my soul

The shepherd provides for his sheep food, drink, and
shelter (Psa. 23:2) and help when they need it (verse 3). Sheep
need physical help. We need both physical and spiritual
help. 'He restores my soul' includes the physical rest and
refreshment that God gives us. 'You let me catch my breath,'
Eugene Peterson translated those words in *The Message*.
Matthew Henry wrote: 'God provides for his people not
only food and rest, but refreshment also and pleasure.'[1] The
Lord revives us when we are weary, troubled, anxious, worn
down with care and work. He gives us new strength and

[1] Henry, *Commentary*, 258.

fills us with fresh joy. But he does much more than that. Derek Kidner writes, 'the retrieving or reviving of the sheep pictures the deeper renewal of the man of God, spiritually perverse or ailing as he may be.'[2] Kenneth Bailey translates the words 'he restores my soul' as 'he brings me back' or 'he causes me to repent.'[3]

After we have been rescued by God, we may wander away. Spurgeon wrote that the Lord's sheep sometimes

> stray from the pastures of truth and holiness. They may fall into gross error, sad sin, and grievous hardness; but yet the Lord, who has become a surety for them to his Father, will not suffer one of them to go so far as to perish. He will by providence and grace pursue them into foreign lands, into abodes of poverty, into dens of obscurity, into deeps of despair; he will not lose one of all that the Father has given him.[4]

In Hosea 11:3 there is a beautiful picture of what God did for the people of Israel who had turned from him and were 'burning offerings to idols.' 'I led them,' God says, 'with cords of kindness, and with bands of love, and I became to them as one who eases the yoke on their jaws, and I bent down to them and fed them.' God not only saves us when we are lost sinners, but he restores us when we are wandering Christians.

Jesus said, 'My sheep hear my voice, and I know them, and they follow me. I give them eternal life, and they will never perish, and no one will snatch them out of my hand'

[2] Kidner, *Psalms 1–72*, 110.
[3] Bailey, *The Good Shepherd*, 45.
[4] Spurgeon, 'April 19,' *Cheque Book of the Bank of Faith*.

(John 10:27, 28). Christ's sheep are his and he will never lose whom he has received from his Father and bought with his own blood. William Plumer summed up what Psalm 23:3 and the whole Bible teaches, 'Unmerited grace will finish what it began.'[5]

SHEEP AND SHEPHERDS

Stewart Perowne quotes these words from a sermon by F. W. Robertson:

> Try to feel, by imagining what the lonely Syrian shepherd must feel towards the helpless things which are the companions of his daily life, for whose safety he stands in jeopardy every hour, and whose value is measurable to him, not by price, but by his own jeopardy, and then we have reached some notion of the love that Jesus meant to represent, that eternal tenderness which bends over us – infinitely lower though we be in nature – and knows the name of each, and thinks for each with a separate solicitude, and gave himself for each with a sacrifice as special, and a love as personal, as if in the whole world's wilderness were none other but that one.[6]

* * *

M. P. Krikorian, the Armenian shepherd who became a pastor, a shepherd of people, writes:

> When the sheep are put forth in the morning each takes its place ... in the grazing line, and keeps the

[5] Plumer, *Psalms*, 312.
[6] Perowne, *Book of Psalms*, 1:250.

same position throughout the day. When tending my sheep I wondered much at this. Once during the day each sheep would break away from the line and, approaching the shepherd with an expectant eye, lift a mild 'baa' or 'huh, huh.' The shepherd knows the meaning of this ... [and] by holding out his hand encourages the sheep and the sheep runs to him. The shepherd then rubs its nose and ears, scratches its chin, strokes his hand over its back with a few gentle taps on the shoulder, whispers love words into its ears, 'How do you like your shepherd? Did you enjoy your food today? Any briars or thorns, or snake bites?' And he fondles it affectionately. The sheep, in the meantime, rubs against the shepherd's leg, telling him with all its strength that it loves him, or, if the shepherd be sitting down, nibbles at his ears, the ears that are ever open to its cry, and rubs its cheek like a true lover against the face of the faithful herder. After a few moments of such communion and exchange of love and friendship with the master, and finding fullness of joy in his presence, the sheep returns to its place in the feeding line refreshed and made content by the personal contact with the shepherd.[7]

PRAYERS, QUOTATIONS, AND STORIES

I have gone astray like a lost sheep; seek your servant,
    for I do not forget your commandments.

(Psa. 119:176)

---

[7] Meshach Paul Krikorian, *The Spirit of the Shepherd: An Interpretation of the Psalm Immortal* (Philadelphia: Krikorian, 1950), 87-88.

'The General Confession' in *The Book of Common Prayer*:

> Almighty and most merciful Father; we have erred, and strayed from thy ways like lost sheep. We have followed too much the devices and desires of our own hearts. We have offended against thy holy laws. We have left undone those things which we ought to have done; and we have done those things which we ought not to have done; and there is no health in us. But thou, O Lord, have mercy upon us, miserable offenders. Spare thou those, O God, who confess their faults. Restore thou those who are penitent; according to thy promises declared unto mankind in Christ Jesus our Lord. And grant, O most merciful Father, for his sake; that we may hereafter live a godly, righteous, and sober life. To the glory of thy holy Name. Amen.

* * *

Charles Kingsley wrote: 'Jesus understood the weakness of his sheep by being weak himself; understood the sorrows of his sheep by sorrowing himself; understood the sins of his sheep by bearing all their sins; understood the temptations of his sheep by conquering [the temptations] himself.'[8]

* * *

[8] Quoted in Isabel Anders, *Walking with the Shepherd* (Nashville: Thomas Nelson, 1994), 40-41.

In *Diary of an Old Soul*, George MacDonald wrote:

> Things go not wrong when sudden I fall prone,
> But when I snatch my upheld hand from thine,
> And, proud or careless, think to walk alone.
> Then things go wrong, when I, poor, silly sheep,
> To shelves and pits from the good pasture creep;
> Not when the shepherd leaves the ninety and nine,
> And to the mountains goes, after the foolish one.[9]

* * *

In his novel *Black Rock: A Tale of the Selkirks*, Ralph Connor tells about a man talking to a boy who was worried sick over something he had done. 'Listen, Billy,' the man said, 'do you remember the sheep that got lost over the mountains? The shepherd didn't beat it when he got it, did he? He took it in his arms and carried it home. And so he will you.'

MY TESTIMONY

At times I have wandered away from the Lord, like Christian and Hopeful did in *The Pilgrim's Progress* when they left their rough path for a more appealing one in By-Path Meadow. My six-year old granddaughter and I were drawing, and I messed up my picture. Zoe said, 'Don't worry. I can turn a mistake into a flower.' And she did! God can do something about my sins. He throws our sins behind his back (Isa. 38:17), so that he would no longer see them. He casts 'all our sins into the depths of the sea' (Mic. 7:19).

[9] George MacDonald, *Diary of an Old Soul* (Minneapolis: Augsburg, 1975), 95.

He says, 'I have blotted out your transgressions like a cloud and your sins like mist' (Isa. 45:22). 'As far as the east is from the west' – an infinite distance – 'so far does he remove our transgressions from us' (Psa. 103:12).

The Moravians prayed, 'Thank you for remembering me, and not my sins. Thank you that you do not instil guilt and shame. Forgive me for carrying a burden of past deeds. Help me to lay them at your cross.'

Christians have a theology of failure. 'If we say we have no sin, we deceive ourselves, and the truth is not in us' (1 John 1:8). But we also have a theology of recovery. 'If we confess our sins, he is faithful and just to forgive us our sins and to cleanse us from all unrighteousness' (1 John 1:9). Fleming Rutledge writes, 'The mighty theme of the Scriptures is God's continual overriding of our failures to accomplish his purpose for good.'[10]

My wife, Anne, says that her favourite part of Psalm 23 are the words 'He restores my soul.' 'I can't do it,' she says. 'I can't even begin to do it, but my Shepherd can restore me and that is what he does.'

> O to grace how great a debtor
>   Daily I'm constrained to be;
> Let that grace now, like a fetter,
>   Bind my wand'ring heart to thee.
> Prone to wander – Lord, I feel it –
>   Prone to leave the God I love:
> Here's my heart, O take and seal it,
>   Seal it for thy courts above.
>
> (Robert Robinson, 1735–90)

[10] Fleming Rutledge, *Help My Unbelief* (Grand Rapids: Eerdmans, 2000), 57.

FOUR

HE LEADS ME IN PATHS OF RIGHTEOUSNESS FOR HIS NAME'S SAKE.

DOROTHY ANN THRUPP

1836

Saviour, like a shepherd lead us,
  Much we need thy tender care;
In thy pleasant pastures feed us,
  For our use thy folds prepare:
Blessed Jesus, blessed Jesus,
  Thou hast bought us, thine we are.

We are thine; do thou befriend us,
  Be the guardian of our way;
Keep thy flock, from sin defend us,
  Seek us when we go astray:
Blessed Jesus, blessed Jesus,
  Hear, O hear us when we pray.

Thou hast promised to receive us,
  Poor and sinful though we be;

Thou hast mercy to relieve us,
  Grace to cleanse, and pow'r to free:
Blessed Jesus, blessed Jesus,
  Let us early turn to thee.

Early let us seek thy favour;
  Early let us do thy will;
Blessed Lord and only Saviour,
  With thy love our bosoms fill:
Blessed Jesus, blessed Jesus,
  Thou hast loved us, love us still.

DOROTHY ANN THRUPP was a British hymn writer and
translator. Many of her hymns were written especially for
children. 'Saviour, Like a Shepherd Lead Us' first appeared
in her collection *Hymns for the Young* in 1836.

COMMENTARY

He leads me in paths of righteousness

The shepherd leads his sheep in the best paths for
food, water, and safety. What does it mean when the Good
Shepherd leads us 'in paths of righteousness'? Two ideas are
expressed by these words.

First, 'paths of righteousness' refers to wise and righteous paths, as in Proverbs 2:6-11:

> For the LORD gives wisdom; from his mouth come
> knowledge and understanding; he stores up sound
> wisdom for the upright; he is a shield to those who walk
> in integrity, guarding the paths of justice and watching
> over the way of his saints. Then you will understand
> righteousness and justice and equity; every good path;

for wisdom will come into your heart and knowledge will be pleasant to your soul; discretion will watch over you, understanding will guard you.

Second, 'paths of righteousness' means 'right paths,' given as an alternative reading in the English Standard Version. Kenneth Bailey writes that 'the classical Armenian translation from the early fifth century reads, "He brings me from the wrong path to the right path."'[1] The 'path of righteousness" is the path of God's will for my life. 'You make known to me the path of life; in your presence there is fullness of joy; at your right hand are pleasures forevermore' (Psa. 16:11).

'Right paths' – those that go in the right direction and those that describe right conduct – are the same paths. The direction of God for my life is also the way of integrity, justice, and equity. David, who wrote in Psalm 23:3, 'He leads me in paths of righteousness,' prayed in Psalm 25:4, 5, 'Make me to know your ways, O LORD; teach me your paths. Lead me in your truth and teach me.'

For his name's sake

George Lamsa writes that 'the shepherd is very careful about the paths because he loves the sheep, and for his own name's sake he will do anything to prevent accidents and attacks by animals. He has to keep his reputation as a good shepherd.'[2] We noted in the first sentence of Psalm 23 that God's name is 'LORD.' He is the compassionate and covenant-keeping God. His wise and loving purposes for

[1] Bailey, *The Good Shepherd*, 44.
[2] Quoted by Bailey, *The Good Shepherd*, 46.

his creation are guaranteed by his name. David writes in Psalm 138:2, 'I bow down toward your holy temple and give thanks to your name for your steadfast love and your faithfulness, for you have exalted above all things your name and your word.' God's covenant promises are clear and his faithfulness to those promises is sure.

> Great is thy faithfulness, O God my father;
>   there is no shadow of turning with thee;
> thou changest not, thy compassions they fail not;
>   as thou hast been thou forever wilt be.
>   (Thomas O. Chisholm, 1866–1960)

David prays: 'For your name's sake, O LORD, preserve my life! In your righteousness bring my soul out of trouble!' (Psa. 143:11). 'Thus says the Lord GOD: It is not for your sake, O house of Israel, that I am about to act, but for the sake of my holy name' (Ezek. 36:22). 'What is at stake in life is the fulfilment not of the human will but of the divine will, so that God's name, his glory, and his wisdom may be extolled.'[3] 'This song of trust [Psalm 23] celebrates I AM's competence, not the sheep's efforts.'[4] 'Our ultimate destiny is not dependent upon our godliness; it is dependent upon God's own nature.'[5]

---

[3] Artur Weiser, *The Psalms* (Philadelphia: Westminster Press, 1962), 229.

[4] Waltke & Houston, *The Psalms as Christian Worship*, 439.

[5] Rutledge, *Help My Unbelief*, 181.

SHEEP AND SHEPHERDS

George Lamsa writes:

> As a boy, I was trained to feed the lambs and sometimes was a shepherd's helper. My father had also spent many years of his life as a shepherd and was known as a good shepherd and musician ... Jesus called himself the door of the sheep, that is, the door of the fold where the sheep are housed during the night. Like a good shepherd he gave his life for the sake of the sheep. The Psalmist calls God the Shepherd of Israel, who neither slumbers nor sleeps.

> God's care for his people is like that of a good shepherd for his flock. He is constantly mindful of their daily needs and protection. God leads us to new paths. He comforts our hearts and heals our wounds. He meets the needs of those who trust in him wherever they go for they understand that the Lord is wonderful and lacks nothing. So they never dream of wanting. Just as the sheep hear the voice of the shepherd, God's people hear the voices of prophets and men of God, who direct them to the place of abundance, which is the truth.

> In mountainous regions and hilly country one finds narrow paths trodden by men and sheep. Sometimes the whole mountain, during the grazing season, is full of winding paths, so that it is difficult to know which is the best, safest and shortest path leading to pasture. Sheep have no intuition – as do other animals – to find the right and safe road. They have to be led.[6]

[6] Lamsa, *A Shepherd for All*, 21, 26, 35.

* * *

Stephen Haboush writes:

It is to be remembered that the shepherds of Palestine, from time immemorial, invariably lead their sheep and hardly ever drive them. For two reasons: first, because of the wild beasts, and second, because of the unfenced fields of grain. The pastures and planted fields are divided by narrow paths, and here and there by low stone walls. These stone walls are intended more for landmarks than for fences. During the planting, growing, and ripening of the grain the fields are forbidden ground. Thus, when they move their flocks from one pasture to another, the shepherds must not permit any of their sheep to stray from the beaten paths into the fields. For if they do the shepherds will not only have to pay damages to the owners of the fields, but they will ruin their reputations as shepherds. However, when the harvest of the grain is over they are allowed to enter the fields, but not until then. Now I look back with satisfaction to the fact that, though the fields of temptation were on either side of the paths, yet none of my sheep strayed into them, because they would hear my voice and follow me.[7]

PRAYERS, QUOTATIONS, AND STORIES

When he has brought out all his own, he goes before them, and the sheep follow him, for they know his voice.

(John 10:4)

[7] Haboush, *My Shepherd Life in Galilee*, 65.

* * *

Preaching on Psalm 23, Spurgeon said:

> Look at the past and see how he has guided you. How
> very little you and I have had to do with it after all! We
> have struggled; we have fretted; we have repined; we
> have fumed against the workings of providence; but,
> after all, I do not know that we have had much more to
> do with it than the sheep in the stream has had to do
> with the way in which it has floated to the other side.
> There is far more of the hand of God in our life than
> there is of our own hand, if our life is what it ought
> to be … We can truly say that we have been divinely
> led until now; and although the journey has been like
> that of the children of Israel in the wilderness – in and
> out, backwards and forwards, progressing and then
> retrograding, and often standing still – yet the Lord
> has led us by a right way up to this present moment.[8]

* * *

American Presbyterian missionary Samuel Lapsley
sang, as he and his colleague William Henry Sheppard
[9]trekked a dangerous path into the heart of Africa:

> Wherever he may guide me,
>   No want shall turn me back;
> My Shepherd is beside me,
>   And nothing can I lack.

[8] Spurgeon, *Metropolitan Tabernacle Pulpit*, 52:458-59.
[9] Lapsley and Sheppard's stories are told in David B. Calhoun,
Swift and Beautiful: The Amazing Stories of Faithful Missionaries
(Edinburgh: Banner of Truth Trust, 2020).

His wisdom ever waketh,
　His eyes are never dim;
He knows the way he taketh,
　And I will walk with him.[10]
　　　　　　　　(Anna L. Waring, 1823–1910)

MY TESTIMONY

We did not have a television in our house, so my father and I listened to the radio for the broadcasts of the St Louis Cardinals' baseball games. And I read books. I loved my Bible story book with its colourful pictures. I loved John Bunyan's *Pilgrim's Progress*. My father acquired a filmstrip illustrating the scenes in Bunyan's book, and for almost a year he taught a Bible class in our home using these pictures. Week by week I listened and watched, fascinated and sometimes terrified, as the story unfolded. One picture that I could not forget was that of the man with the muck rake. The poor man was looking down, searching for something of value in the dirt and muck at his feet, while an angel in shining robes stood behind him holding a golden crown. Why would the man not look up? Why would he not turn around and see what he was missing? I was glad that I was not that man, but I felt sorry for him. That picture and many others from *Pilgrim's Progress* shaped my mind and imagination as a child – and still do.

As a child I wanted to be a missionary. Missionaries came to our church and visited our home. They were interesting people who told exciting stories. Mr Bailey, a missionary in Africa, knew all about lions. He could even

[10] From the hymn, 'In Heavenly Love Abiding.'

roar like a lion, which he did at least once in every sermon. When I heard a real lion roar in a zoo I was disappointed. He did not do nearly as well as Mr Bailey!

I went to Columbia Bible College, where there was one major – Bible. I learned a lot about the Bible, and not all that much about anything else. I sometimes regretted not going to the University of South Carolina and studying history and literature, but I know now that Columbia Bible College was the right path for me. It helped me to know the Bible, and nothing has been more important than that in my whole life.

After the Bible College I went to Covenant Seminary in St Louis. I studied under a faculty of competent scholars who were also experienced pastors – Robert G. Rayburn, J. Oliver Buswell, Laird Harris, Wilbur Wallis, and Elmer Smick. Francis Schaeffer, who had moved from a pastorate in St Louis to begin his ministry in Switzerland, returned regularly to give lectures at the seminary. At Columbia Bible College I learned what was in the Bible. At Covenant Seminary I learned that all the Bible from Genesis to Revelation was about one thing – God's covenant grace in Christ.

A week after our wedding, Anne and I arrived in Grand Cayman Island to serve the Boatswain Bay Presbyterian Church during the summer. There were cows wandering through Georgetown, the island's capital, only one paved road, one bank, and no telephones. The mangrove-covered island was swarming with mosquitoes, many of which I swallowed when preaching on Sunday nights as the kerosene lanterns attracted them. Anne and I rode bicycles to visit our church members during the week, and on the Lord's Day we taught Sunday school and I preached twice. Most of the younger men worked on merchant ships, leaving behind a congregation largely of women and children, missing their husbands and fathers, sons, and brothers. We prayed for them and almost every Sunday, as Anne played the old pump organ (with the help of a little boy who did the pumping), we sang the hymn:

> Eternal Father, strong to save,
>   Whose arm doth bind the restless wave,
> Who bidd'st the mighty ocean deep
>   Its own appointed limits keep:
> O hear us when we cry to thee
>   For those in peril on the sea.
>   (William Whiting, 1825–78)

Anne and I spent one summer at L'Abri in Switzerland, studying with Francis Schaeffer. We lived in 'Chalet Bambi,' and our little son, Allen, played happily in the fields around the chalet. I learned from Dr Schaeffer that Christianity was not only about church, Bible study, personal devotions, and witnessing to the lost. All these things are important and indeed essential, but at L'Abri I learned that there is more to Christianity. 'There is not an inch in the entire area of our human life which Christ, who is sovereign of all, does not call "mine,"' said Abraham Kuyper in one of his famous lectures on Calvinism given at Princeton Seminary in 1898. Columbia Bible College taught me the Bible, Covenant Seminary deepened my knowledge of God's word, and study at L'Abri widened it to embrace the whole world.

After teaching at Columbia Bible College for four years, Anne and I returned to the West Indies, to the island of

Jamaica where I was principal of Jamaica Bible College. We loved life in Jamaica – the staple dish of rice and peas, the tropical fruits, the climate in our mountain town of Mandeville, the year-round flowers, and mostly the people. We worshipped at a church that had been founded and served by missionaries from Ireland for over a hundred years. The Rev. Earl Thames, who studied at Oxford as a Rhodes scholar, was the first Jamaican pastor of that church. He baptized our daughter, Isabel, who was born in Jamaica. Earl was a good preacher and a gifted musician. He wrote a Christmas carol in Jamaican patois, set to the well-known West Indian calypso tune 'Yellow Bird.' It began,

> Jesu, Lord, wha' mek you come down to we,
> Leave you home and mix up with such as me?

Our school choir sang that song in its concerts in churches across the island.

After four years in Jamaica, I studied New Testament at Princeton Theological Seminary. A few years later, after more missionary work in the West Indies, and some months of study in Florence, Italy, we went back to Princeton, where I earned a PhD in church history to prepare to teach at Covenant Seminary. I was professor at Covenant for over thirty years. I loved Covenant because of its commitment to the Bible and the *Westminster Confession of Faith*, because of my colleagues on the faculty, and because of my students. What a wonderful group of men and women, of various races, from many parts of this country and from overseas. As I taught them, I learned from them.

The last five years of my active ministry, I served on the pastoral staff of Galilee Baptist Church, an African

American church in downtown St Louis. I preached a farewell sermon at Galilee in 2014, when we were moving from St Louis to Batavia, Illinois, near Chicago, to live near our daughter and her family. My text was Colossians 1:3-8, and my title was 'What I Found at Galilee.' There I found what Paul had learned about the church at Colosse – 'faith in Christ Jesus, love for all the saints, and the hope of heaven.'

In *Out of Africa* Isak Dineson wrote, 'The discovery of the dark races was to me a magnificent enlargement of all my world.'[11] The black people of my hometown in South Carolina, the people of the West Indies, and the African Americans of Galilee Baptist Church were all 'a magnificent enlargement' of my world. I was privileged to sing with my black brothers and sisters at Galilee, especially during Black History Month, James Weldon Johnson's 'Lift Every Voice and Sing,' a hymn that became known as the 'Negro National Anthem.' The last verse is a prayer:

> God of our weary years, God of our silent tears,
>   Thou who hast brought us thus far on the way;
> Thou who hast by thy might, led us into the light,
>   Keep us forever in the path, we pray.

Anne and I sometimes ask each other, 'What would you have done differently? What other choices would you have made?' Looking back over our lives we see that the Lord has led us in the right paths and, though at times one or the other of us hesitated or turned aside, he always brought us back to 'the paths of righteousness for his name's sake.' These were not always the paths we would have chosen, but

---

[11] Quoted by John Updike, *Self-Consciousness: Memoirs* (New York: Alfred A. Knopf, 1989), 66.

they were the right paths for us. 'Ponder the path of your feet; then all your ways will be sure. Do not swerve to the right or to the left; turn your foot away from evil' (Prov. 4:26, 27).

FIVE

EVEN THOUGH I WALK THROUGH THE VALLEY OF THE SHADOW OF DEATH.

HARRY H. BARRY
1855–1919

'*In pastures green?*' Not always. Sometimes
He, who knoweth best, in kindness leadeth me
In weary ways, where heavy shadows be;
Out of the sunshine, warm and soft and bright,
Out of the sunshine into darkest night;
I oft would faint with sorrow and affright;
Only for this – I know he holds my hand,
So whether in a green or desert land,
I trust, although I may not understand.

'*And by still waters?*' No, not always so.
Ofttimes the heavy tempests round me blow,
And o'er my soul the waves and billows go.
But when the storm beats loudest, and I cry
Aloud for help, the Master standeth by
And whispers to my soul: 'Lo! It is I.'
Above the tempest wild I hear him say:

'Beyond this darkness lies the perfect day.
In every path of thine I lead the way.'

So whether on the hilltop high and fair
I dwell, or in the sunless valley where
The shadows lie – what matters? He is there.
And more than this, where'er the pathway
Leads, He gives to me no helpless, broken reed,
But his own hand sufficient for my need.
So where he leadeth I can safely go,
And in the blest hereafter I shall know
Why, in his wisdom, he hath led me so.

THIS little-known poem by Henry H. Barry is found in two devotional books – *Leaves of Healing*, compiled by Katharine Paine Sutton, and *Streams in the Desert*, edited by Mrs Charles E. Cowman.

COMMENTARY

Even though I walk through the valley of the shadow of death

Christian's journey from the City of Destruction to the Celestial City, described by John Bunyan in *The Pilgrim's Progress*, includes many delightful and happy experiences, but there are also times of suffering and fear. Christian visits the 'Delectable Mountains,' and he falls into 'the Slough of Despond.' He comes to 'House Beautiful,' but he has to climb 'Hill Difficulty.' He enjoys 'the Country of Beulah' – where birds sing, flowers are always blooming, and the sun shines night and day. But he soon comes to 'the valley of the shadow of death.'

Christians have many joyful times, but we also experience times of sadness, depression, anxiety, sickness, abuse, or bitter disappointment. Romans 8:35 speaks of the possibility of 'tribulation, or distress, or persecution, or famine, or nakedness, or danger, or the sword.' Like Christian we sooner or later come to 'the valley of the shadow of death,' or, as the Hebrew of Psalm 23:5 may be translated, 'the valley of deep darkness.'

The Psalms enable us to 'think and behave theologically when *in extremis*,' writes Ellen Charry.[1] Psalm 23:4 does this by setting before us two unshakeable facts. It is God who chooses my path, and even when that path leads to a 'valley of deep darkness' it is the right path for me. Derek Kidner writes, 'The dark valley, or ravine, is as truly one of his "right paths" as are the green pastures – a fact that takes much of the sting out of any ordeal.'[2] J. Wilbur Chapman writes:

> Not always beside the gentle streamlet flow, but sometimes by the foaming torrent; not always over the delicate grass, but sometimes up the stony mountain track; not always in the sunshine, but sometimes through the valley of the shadow of death. But whichever it is, it is the right way and it is the way home.[3]

The second great unshakeable fact is that the Lord will be with us every step of the way. We will think more about that in the next chapter.

[1] Ellen T. Charry, *Psalms 1-50: Sighs and Songs of Israel*, in *Brazos Theological Commentary on the Bible* (Grand Rapids: Brazos Press, 2015), xvi.

[2] Kidner, *Psalms 1–72*, 110.

[3] J. Wilbur Chapman, *The Secret of a Happy Day: Quiet Hour Meditations* (Boston and Chicago: United Society of Christian Endeavour, 1899), 61-62.

Sheep and Shepherds

M. P. Krikorian wrote:

> There is an actual valley of the shadow of death [just south of the Jerusalem-Jericho road] in Palestine, and every shepherd knows of it … It is a very narrow defile through a mountain range where the water often foams and roars, torn by jagged rocks … The path plunges downward from about twenty-seven hundred feet above sea level at one end to nearly four hundred feet below sea level at the other, into a deep and narrow gorge of sheer precipices overhung by frowning Sphinx-like battlements of rocks, which almost touch overhead … The valley is about five miles long, yet it is not more than twelve feet at the widest section of the base. The valley of flaming purple rocks is made perilous and dangerous not only through vicious animals that crouch in their dens and lie in wait in their covert, and deadly snakes lurking among the rocks, but because of its furrowed floor, badly eroded by the floods and waters from cloudbursts. The actual path, on the solid rock, is so narrow that in places the sheep can hardly turn around in case of danger.[4]

Prayers, Quotations, and Stories

> Who shall separate us from the love of Christ? Shall tribulation, or distress, or persecution, or famine, or nakedness, or danger, or the sword?
>
> (Rom. 8:35)

* * *

[4] Krikorian, *The Spirit of the Shepherd*, 98-99.

On the opening page of *The Shepherd and His Flock*, Church of Scotland minister John R. MacDuff (1818–95) quotes these lines from Thomas Aquinas:

> Good and tender Shepherd, hear us.
>   Bread of Heaven, in love come near us.
> Feed us, lead us, and defend us;
>   Make us see whate'er thou send us,
> In the land of earthly living,
>   Is thy wise and gracious giving.

* * *

Within a year of his unexpected victory in the 400 metres race in the 1924 Olympic Games in Paris, Eric Liddell left Scotland to serve as a missionary in China. He taught at a Christian college for a few years and then entered the arduous work of rural evangelism. As conditions in China worsened during the Second World War, Liddell sent his pregnant wife and two children to Canada, expecting to follow some months later. But before he could leave China, the Japanese armies rounded up all 'enemy nationals' for internment. Eighteen hundred people, including many children, were packed into a small, miserable compound. Eric Liddell's Christlike life and self-denying service blessed and encouraged his fellow prisoners. Liddell taught them to sing his favourite hymn:

> Be still, my soul: the Lord is on thy side;
>   Bear patiently the cross of grief or pain.
> Leave to thy God to order and provide;
>   In every change he faithful will remain.
> Be still, my soul: thy best, thy heavenly friend
>   Through thorny ways leads to a joyful end.
>   (Katharina von Schlegel, 1697–1768)

Eric Liddell died of a brain tumour in 1945, days before he would have been released from the internment camp.

* * *

> For all your blessings, Heavenly Father, known to me, and for all unknown, accept my thanks. May I not murmur at your providence, or dread the future. Whatever happens, help me to believe in your unfailing care and to know that in the Valley of the Shadow you are by my side.[5]

My Testimony

Dante began the *Divine Comedy*, 'Half-way through the journey of my life I found myself in a dark forest.' On Thanksgiving Day 1987 I entered a 'valley of deep darkness.' I was fifty years old.

For some years the Lord had been getting me ready for this valley. Early in 1981 Dr Robert Rayburn, the founding president of Covenant Seminary, told us in chapel that his cancer, which five years earlier had so unexpectedly disappeared, had returned. After a short, frank, moving account of his condition, he asked us to stand and sing a hymn he had chosen. With Dr Rayburn playing the piano, we sang:

> Whate'er my God ordains is right;
>   His holy will abideth;
> I will be still whate'er he doth,
>   And follow where he guideth.
> He is my God; though dark my road,
>   He holds me that I shall not fall:
> Wherefore to him I leave it all.

[5] Meyer, *Daily Prayers*, Prayer for May 3.

Whate'er my God ordains is right:
  Here shall my stand be taken;
Though sorrow, need, or death be mine,
  Yet am I not forsaken.
My Father's care is round me there;
  He holds me that I shall not fall:
And so to him I leave it all.
                    (Samuel Rodigast, 1649–1708)

Dr Rayburn wrote to his friend Francis Schaeffer with
the news of his relapse. Dr Schaeffer, who was also suffering
from cancer, answered from Switzerland:

Dear Bob,

Thank you for your letter. It was good to have the
news directly from you. Of course, both you and I
know that unless the Lord heals us completely that
once we have faced the question of cancer we always
must also face the possibility of its recurrence. With
modern medicine, and I am sure prayer very much
does go hand in hand with it, there is a possibility of
the thing being controlled even if the Lord does not
heal us completely. I would not write to anybody else
like this but both you and I have faced the thing plus
having our faith fixed in the Lord in some sort of
stable fashion!

If I could wave a wand and be rid of the lymphoma I
would do it. Yet in my own case looking back over the
whole two and half years since I have known I have
lymphoma, there has been more that has been positive
than negative. That is true on many levels and I am not
just thinking of some vague concept of understanding people better, though I guess that is true as well.
Rather, in the total complex of everything that has

happened I am convinced that there is more positive than negative. I am also increasingly conscious of the fact that Edith and I have been, as it were, carried along on an escalator for the entirety of our lives. I am left in awe and wonder with all this, and I very much feel the escalator is still in operation, not just in this matter of health, but in the battles that beset us on every side.

In the Lamb,

Fran.[6]

During the fall semester of 1987 I was preaching in the seminary chapel a series of sermons on the book of Habakkuk. I had preached on the first two chapters, and I was scheduled to preach on chapter 3. That concluding chapter is not about the prophet's complaints and questions that we find in chapters 1 and 2. It is a song of trust in God no matter what happens.

> Though the fig tree should not blossom, nor fruit be on the vines, the produce of the olive fails and there are no grapes on the vines, though the olive crop fails and the fields produce no food, though there are no sheep in the pen and no cattle in the stalls, yet I will rejoice in the Lord; I will take joy in the God of my salvation (Hab. 3:17, 18).

As I was preparing to preach on Habakkuk chapter 3, I discovered a little lump in my neck. I went to the doctor who ordered a biopsy. He told me not to worry, most likely it was nothing serious. I, of course, was hoping for good news, but with Habakkuk's testimony in my mind I was prepared if the news was bad. I prayed that Psalm 112:7

[6] Dr Schaeffer died in 1984, and Dr Rayburn, early in 1990.

would be true of me: 'He is not afraid of bad news; his heart is firm, trusting in the LORD.'

I preached on Habakkuk 3, and concluded the chapel service with William Cowper's hymn:

Sometimes a light surprises
  The Christian while he sings;
It is the Lord, who rises
  With healing in his wings:
When comforts are declining,
  He grants the soul again
A season of clear shining,
  To cheer it after rain.

In holy contemplation
  We sweetly then pursue
The theme of God's salvation,
  And find it ever new;
Set free from present sorrow,
  We cheerfully can say,
'Let the unknown tomorrow
  Bring with it what it may.'

Though vine nor fig tree neither
  Their wonted fruit shall bear,
Though all the fields should wither,
  Nor flocks nor herds be there;
Yet God the same abideth,
  His praise shall tune my voice,
For, while in him confiding,
  I cannot but rejoice.

On Thanksgiving Day, my doctor called to tell me that I had a relatively rare form of non-Hodgkins lymphoma, a cancer almost always fatal within five years. Even today less than ten percent of people with mantle cell lymphoma have lived ten years.

Soon I was sick from the brutal effects of chemotherapy. I prayed in the words of the psalmist, 'Oh my God, take me not away in the midst of my days' (Psa. 102:24).

When radiation to my throat burned my vocal cords and I could no longer teach my classes, I felt useless. Words by C. S. Lewis helped me:

> We must not fret about not doing God those supposed services which He in fact does not allow us to do. Very often I expect, the service He really demands is that of not being (apparently) used, or not in the way we expected, or not in a way we can perceive.[7]

Elihu was wrong about Job but right about God when he said that God 'gives songs in the night' (Job 35:10). 'There is great beauty in this expression,' wrote Albert Barnes.[8] 'It has been verified in thousands of instances where the afflicted have looked up through tears to God, and their mourning has been turned into joy.' One of my most-loved 'songs in the night' was:

> He giveth more grace when the burdens grow greater,
> He sendeth more strength when the labours increase;
> To added affliction he addeth his mercy,
> To multiplied trials, his multiplied peace.

[7] C. S. Lewis, *Letters to an American Lady* (Grand Rapids: Eerdmans, 1967), 72.

[8] Albert Barnes, *Notes on the Old Testament: The Book of Job* (1847; repr. Grand Rapids: Baker, 1987), 2:176.

His love has no limit, his grace has no measure,
His power has no boundary known unto men;
For out of his infinite riches in Jesus,
He giveth, and giveth, and giveth again!
　　　　　　　(Annie Johnson Flint, 1866–1932)

The cancer that began in my neck spread to my throat and then to the colon, requiring over fifty colonoscopies during the next twenty-five years. Occasionally, my cancer would be in remission for a year or two, but it always returned. After I retired from teaching at Covenant Seminary, Anne and I moved from St Louis to the Chicago area to be near our daughter and her family. My new oncologist told a colleague, also a cancer specialist, 'I have a patient who has had mantle cell lymphoma for over thirty years.' The friend replied, 'No, you don't! That's not possible.'

In 1996 I wrote a letter to the seminary community, ending with these words:

> On one occasion the Psalmist wrote, 'I will not die but live, and proclaim what the LORD has done' (Psa. 118:17). I cannot know whether that verse will be true of me at this time in my life, but there is another verse that I am absolutely sure about. 'If we live, we live to the Lord; and if we die, we die to the Lord. So whether we live or die, we belong to the Lord' (Rom. 14:8).

The apostle Paul was sure about that. So was Richard Baxter. When his wife died, Baxter wrote an account of her life in which he described a covenant she had made with God. He turned her words into verse:

> Lord, it belongs not to my care
> Whether I die or live;

To love and serve thee is my share,
    And this thy grace must give.

If life be long, I will be glad,
    That I may long obey;
If short, then why should I be sad
    To soar to endless day?

Come Lord, when grace has made me meet
    Thy blessed face to see;
For if thy work on earth be sweet,
    What will thy glory be?

I was reading Calvin's *Sermons on the Beatitudes* when, on Good Friday, April 6, 2007, I received a call from a doctor that a recent colonoscopy showed that my cancer had returned after almost two years of remission. I had just read the following words from John Calvin – words that I returned to again and again during the next few days. Calvin wrote:

> While life for believers may be easy today, they will be ready tomorrow to endure whatever afflictions God may send them. He may, perhaps, take from them the goods he has given. They are prepared to surrender them, since they know they received them on one condition – that they should hand them back whenever God should choose. The believer reasons this way: 'Rich today, poor tomorrow.' If God should change my circumstances so that ease gives way to suffering and laughter to tears, it is enough to know that I am still his child. He has promised to acknowledge me always as his, and in that I rest content.[9]

[9] John Calvin, tr. Robert White, *Sermons on the Beatitudes*, (Edinburgh: Banner of Truth Trust, 2006), 78.

SIX

I WILL FEAR NO EVIL, FOR YOU ARE WITH ME; YOUR ROD AND YOUR STAFF THEY COMFORT ME.

FANNY J. CROSBY

1875

All the way my Saviour leads me;
　What have I to ask beside?
Can I doubt his tender mercy,
　Who through life has been my guide?
Heav'nly peace, divinest comfort,
　Here by faith in him to dwell;
For I know, whate'er befall me,
　Jesus doeth all things well.

All the way my Saviour leads me,
　Cheers each winding path I tread,
Gives me grace for ev'ry trial,
　Feeds me with the living bread.
Though my weary steps may falter,
　And my soul athirst may be,

Gushing from the rock before me,
    Lo, a spring of joy I see.

All the way my Saviour leads me—
    O the fullness of his love!
Perfect rest to me is promised
    In my Father's house above:
When my spirit, clothed immortal,
    Wings its flight to realms of day,
This my song through endless ages:
    Jesus led me all the way.

FANNY CROSBY was born in New York State in 1823. As a baby she lost her sight because of a medical mistake. During her lifetime she wrote hundreds of hymns, of which sixty or more are still used. These include 'Safe in the Arms of Jesus,' 'To God Be the Glory,' and 'All the Way My Saviour Leads Me.' The testimony of the blind poet is expressed in her hymns, especially in the words of the hymn quoted above – 'Jesus led me all the way!'

COMMENTARY

I will fear no evil, for you are with me

Sheep are comforted by knowing that in the most dangerous and alarming places their shepherd is with them. God does not promise that we will face no evil; he promises that we need fear no evil. Stewart Perowne writes that Psalm 23 'speaks of a peace so deep, a serenity so profound, that even the thought of the shadow of death cannot trouble it.'[1] Patrick Miller says that the words of Psalm 23:4 are

[1] Perowne, *Book of Psalms*, 1:248.

the gospel kernel of the Old Testament, that good news that turns tears of anguish and fears into shouts of joy, that glad tidings given by the angelic choir to the shepherds, which itself echoes a word first given to the patriarchs and repeated again and again to Israel in moments of distress and fear: You don't have to be afraid. This is the salvation word par excellence of Scripture, Old Testament as well as New.[2]

There is a dramatic change in the language of verse 4 of Psalm 23 from the third to the second person. In the first three verses David had written: 'He makes me lie down in green pastures'; 'He leads me beside still waters'; 'He restores my soul'; 'He leads me in paths of righteousness.' But in verse 4 David writes, 'You are with me.' When things are going well we may be content to talk about the Lord; but when we approach the valley of the shadow of death, and the sky darkens and the thunder rolls, we hurry to speak directly to him.

David wrote, 'Even though I walk through the valley of the shadow of death, I will fear no evil, for you are with me.' Another psalmist wrote, 'Nevertheless' – despite the evil all around me – 'I am continually with you; you hold my right hand' (Psa. 73:23). In the valley of the shadow of death the Lord is not in front of me, not behind me, but beside me, close to me, and he holds my hand. 'The darker the shadow, the closer the Lord,' writes Alec Motyer.[3] In several medical procedures I undergo periodically, one of the nurses takes

[2] Patrick D. Miller, *Interpreting the Psalms* (Philadelphia: Fortress Press, 1986), 115.
[3] J. A. Motyer, Psalm 23 in *New Bible Commentary, 21st Century Edition* (Grand Rapids: Eerdmans, 1970), 500.

my hand when the pain is at its worst and says 'squeeze hard.' Holding God's strong hand makes the most difficult times in the valley bearable. George MacDonald ended a poem with these lines:

> Then into his hand went mine,
>   And into my heart came he;
> And I walk in a light divine,
>   The path I had feared to see.

In the valley the Lord is not only beside me but he is also inside me ('into my heart came he') to give me strength to take the next step. 'Seek the LORD and his strength; seek his presence continually!' (Psa. 105:4) Spurgeon wrote: 'Did you ever notice Isaiah 58:9: 'Then you shall call, and the LORD will answer; you shall cry, and he will say, "Here I am." There the Lord seems to put himself at the disposal of his people, saying to them, "Here I am." As much as to say, "What have you to say to me? What can I do for you? I am waiting to bless you"'[4]

Your rod and your staff, they comfort me

David, an experienced shepherd, tells God that in the valley of the shadow of death 'your rod and your staff comfort me.' John Goldingay translates the words 'club and cane.'[5] Unlike most other animals, sheep have no way to defend themselves. They cannot fight. They cannot run. They cannot hide. Their only security is the shepherd.

---

[4] Spurgeon, 'March 27,' *Cheque Book of the Bank of Faith.*
[5] John Goldingay, *Psalms for Everyone, Part 1: Psalms 1-72,* (Philadelphia: Westminster John Knox Press, 2014), 74.

According to Philip Keller, the rod (or club) was 'an extension of the owner's right arm. It stood as a symbol of his strength, his power, his authority in any serious situation.'[6] Our all-powerful Shepherd is able to handle any crisis. 'Great is our Lord, and abundant in power' (Psa. 147:5).

With a long staff (or cane) the shepherd gently keeps the sheep on the right path. He uses it to pick up fallen sheep and get them on their feet again. 'The LORD is good to all, and his mercy is over all that he has made … The LORD upholds all who are falling and raises up all who are bowed down' (Psa. 145:9, 14). 'Shepherd your people with your staff, the flock of your inheritance,' writes the prophet Micah (7:14).

The shepherd's rod and staff comfort the sheep even when they are used for correction, just as God's discipline is a comfort to us. 'Blessed is the man whom you discipline, O LORD, and whom you teach out of your law' (Psa. 94:12). Dietrich Bonhoeffer wrote, 'It is grace to know God's commands. They release us from self-made plans and conflicts. They make our steps certain and our way joyful.'[7] 'For the commandment is a lamp and the teaching a light, and the reproofs of discipline are the way of life' (Prov. 6:23).

When we enter the valley of the shadow of death, with trials and fears around us, and death threatening us, we are faced with a mystery but a 'luminous mystery.'[8] We know

[6] W. Philip Keller, *A Shepherd Looks at Psalm 23* (Grand Rapids: Zondervan, 1970), 84.

[7] Dietrich Bonhoeffer, *Psalms: The Prayer Book of the Bible* (Minneapolis: Augsburg, 1970), 31-32.

[8] Billings, *Rejoicing in Lament*, 72.

that the path through the valley is God's plan for us. We know it is a path, hard but sure, going to some place good. We know, as Spurgeon said, that 'it is a happy thing to be afflicted towards heaven.'[9]

> May my every cross be sanctified,
>   every loss be gain,
>   every denial a spiritual advantage,
>   every dark day a light of the Holy Spirit,
>   every night of trial a song.[10]

SHEEP AND SHEPHERDS

George Lamsa writes:

> Sheep, more than other animals, are easily frightened, especially when passing through strange country at dusk. They are so timid that even the sound of unfamiliar noises and echoes disturbs them. Not having any other way to protect themselves from their natural enemies, their whole trust is placed upon the shepherd they know, and whose presence is always comforting, and whose absence creates fear and disturbance. While grazing, the sheep constantly watch to see that the shepherd is with them, and if they fail to find him, the whole flock is alarmed and scatters ... Even when the sheep are in the fold, the shepherd's presence is needed to keep them quiet. The shepherd and his assistant walk constantly in turns around the fold so that the sheep may sleep and rest in tranquillity.[11]

[9] Spurgeon, *Metropolitan Tabernacle Pulpit*, 27:239.
[10] 'Spiritual Helps,' *The Valley of Vision*.
[11] Lamsa, *The Shepherd of All*, 39.

* * *

In *A Psalm of an Old Shepherd*, Frank Crossley Morgan tells about an experience a friend had while travelling in Palestine.

> In talking to an old shepherd he inquired in what sense it could be said that his staff was for the comfort of the sheep. The old shepherd proceeded to explain that in daylight he always carried the staff across his shoulder, and when the sheep saw it, it spoke of the presence of the shepherd, and thus was a means of comfort. On the other hand if night overtook him with the sheep on the mountainside, or if they were caught in a heavy mountain mist so that the sheep could no longer see the staff, then he would lower it, and as he walked he would tap with it on the ground, so that by hearing, if not by sight, the staff comforted the sheep by speaking of the presence of the shepherd[12]

* * *

William Thomson writes:

> The shepherd goes before, not merely to point out the way, but to see that it is practical and safe. He is armed in order to defend his charge; and in this he is very courageous. Many adventures with wild beasts occur not unlike that recounted by David (1 Sam. 17:34-36), and in these very mountains; for, though there are no lions here, there are wolves in abundance; and leopards and panthers, exceeding fierce, prowl about these wild wadis. They not unfrequently attack the flock in the very presence of the shepherd, and he must be ready

[12] Morgan, *A Psalm of an Old Shepherd*, 48-49.

to do battle at a moment's warning. I have listened with intense interest to their graphic descriptions of downright and desperate fights with these savage beasts. And when the thief and the robber come (and come they do), the faithful shepherd has often to put his life in his hand to defend his flock. I have known more than one case in which he had literally to lay it down in the contest.

The shepherd invariably carries a staff or rod with him when he goeth forth to feed his flock. It is often bent or hooked at one end ... With this staff he rules and guides the flock to their green pastures, and defends them from their enemies. With it, also, he corrects them when disobedient, and brings them back when wandering. This staff is associated as inseparably with the shepherd as the goad is with the ploughman.[13]

PRAYERS, QUOTATIONS, AND STORIES

When you pass through the waters, I will be with you; and through the rivers, they shall not overwhelm you; when you walk through the fire you shall not be burned, and the flame shall not consume you.

(Isa. 43:2)

* * *

In his biography, *Grace Like a River*, Christopher Parkening, world-renowned classical guitarist, says: 'The will of God, I have discovered, will never take me where the grace

---

[13] Thomson, *The Land and the Book*, 205.

of God cannot keep me, protect me, sustain me, calm my fears and teach me.'[14]

* * *

Preaching on Psalm 23 at the Annual Conference of the Evangelical Movement of Wales at Aberystwyth in 1979, J. Douglas MacMillan said:

Somebody said to me last night, 'I am sure, Mr MacMillan, you have noticed that there are only two negatives in this psalm.' Well, I have been looking at this psalm a long time, but I never particularly noticed this. How on earth did I miss them? 'I will not want,' and 'I will fear no evil.' What wonderful negatives they are![15]

* * *

In *The Cheque Book of the Bank of Faith*, C. H. Spurgeon wrote, 'Up to this hour I have suffered no real damage from my many afflictions. I have neither lost faith, nor hope, nor love. Nay, so far from losing these … they have gained in strength and energy. I have more knowledge, more experience, more patience, more stability than I had before the trials came. Not even my joy has been destroyed.'[16]

* * *

[14] Christopher Parkening, *Grace Like a River* (Carol Stream, IL: Tyndale House, 2006), 205.

[15] J. Douglas MacMillan, *The Lord Our Shepherd* (Bryntirion: Evangelical Press of Wales, 1983), 73.

[16] Spurgeon, 'December 19,' *Cheque Book of the Bank of Faith*.

Horatius and Jane Bonar lost three of their children in 1869. 'A hymn that has brought blessing to many others may well have come from this trial,' writes Faith Cook.[17]

> Thy way, not mine, O Lord,
>   However dark it be!
> Lead me by thine own hand;
>   Choose out the path for me.
>
> Take thou my cup, and it
>   With joy or sorrow fill,
> As best to thee may seem:
>   Choose thou my good and ill.

* * *

Gilbert J. Greene recalled an incident involving Abraham Lincoln, then a young lawyer in Springfield, Illinois. Greene and Lincoln rode out into the country together to witness the will of a dying woman. After the business was over, the woman asked Lincoln to read to her from the Bible.

> They offered him the Book, but he did not take it, but began reciting from memory the Twenty-third Psalm, laying special emphasis upon 'Though I walk through the valley of the shadow of death, I will fear no evil, for thou art with me, thy rod and thy staff they comfort me.' Without using the Book, he took up the first of the fourteenth chapter of John – 'In my Father's house are many mansions.' After he had given these and other quotations from the Scriptures, he recited several

[17] Faith Cook, *Our Hymn Writers and Their Hymns* (Darlington: EP Books, 2015), 303.

hymns, closing with 'Rock of Ages, Cleft for Me' ...
The woman was more sick than we realized, and
died while we were there. Riding home, I expressed
surprise that he should have acted as pastor as well
as attorney so perfectly, and Mr Lincoln replied, 'God
and eternity and heaven are very near to me today.'[18]

My Testimony

I will write more in the next chapter about what I
learned in the valley, but here I will say with Abraham
Lincoln, 'God and eternity and heaven are very near to me
today.' And, through my many years of cancer, I can testify
with C. H. Spurgeon, 'I have suffered no real damage ... I
have lost neither faith nor hope nor love.'

[18] Quoted in William L. Holladay, *The Psalms through Three
Thousand Years: Prayerbook of a Cloud of Witnesses* (Minneapolis:
Fortress Press, 1995), 361.

SEVEN

WHAT I LEARNED IN THE VALLEY.

ANDERS C. ARREBO

1587–1637

The Lord my faithful Shepherd is,
　　And me he safely guideth;
I shall not want, for I am his
　　Who all things good provideth.
I follow him, I hear his voice,
　　In him my Lord I do rejoice –
Blest am I in his keeping!

A tender shepherd leads his sheep
　　Where pastures green are growing,
And there his flock doth guard and keep
　　Beside still waters flowing.
Thus Christ, my Shepherd, leadeth me,
　　My soul and body feedeth he
And for their wants provideth.

And if I ever go astray,
　　My wayward soul he turneth,
To save the lost, to guide the way,
　　For this he ever yearneth;

He leadeth me, my soul to bless
  In his own path of righteousness
For his name's sake and glory.

Why should I ever fear, O Lord,
  Whil'st thee I have beside me?
Thou by thy Spirit and thy word
  Dost comfort and dost guide me.
In death's dark vale I'll fear no ill,
  For thou, O Lord, art with me still,
Thy rod and staff shall stay me.

Thou art my host; for me, thy guest,
  A table thou providest.
Though foes be near, I am at rest,
  Thou still with me abidest.
With oil anointest thou my head,
  On me thy blessing rich is shed,
My cup with bliss o'erfloweth.

Thy goodness and thy mercy, Lord,
  Shall follow me, attending
The days thou dost to me afford
  Until they reach their ending.
Thereafter shall I in thy love
  Dwell in thy house in heav'n above
Forever and forever.

ANDERS C. ARREBO was one of the first Lutheran pastors in Denmark.

* * *

Teach me your way, O LORD, that I may walk in your truth; unite my heart to fear your name.

(Psa. 86:11)

What I learned in the valley

Flannery O'Connor, who died of lupus at the age of thirty-nine, said that 'sickness is a place more instructive than a long trip to Europe … Sickness before death is a very appropriate thing and I think those who don't have it miss one of God's mercies.'[1] 'Sickness is a sacred thing,' wrote J. C. Ryle, 'and one of God's great ordinances.'[2]

Christians of old prayed, '… from sudden death, Good Lord deliver us.'[3] They wanted time to prepare for death. *Holy Living and Holy Dying* by Jeremy Taylor, seventeenth-century Church of England bishop, is the most famous of many books treating preparation for death. One of the Puritans prayed, 'May I be increasingly prepared for life's remaining duties, the solemnities of a dying hour, and the joys and services that lie beyond the grave.'[4] Eight days before he died, John Donne wrote a 'Hymn to God, My God, in My Sickness.' It begins:

> Since I am coming to that holy room,
> Where, with thy choir of saints forevermore
> I shall be made thy music, as I come
> I tune the instrument here at the door,
> And what I must do then, think here before.

John Donne, the Puritans, and other Christians wanted the opportunity to speak, as it were, from the very door of

[1] Flannery O'Connor, *Letters of Flannery O'Connor: The Habit of Being* (New York: Farrar, Straus and Giroux, 1979), 163.

[2] J. C. Ryle, *The Power and Sympathy of Christ* (Edinburgh: Banner of Truth Trust, 2018), 11.

[3] From 'The Litany,' *Book of Common Prayer*.

[4] 'Requests,' *The Valley of Vision*.

heaven, to family and friends, to the church, and to the lost. *Fraser: Not a Private Matter* is the story of a young Scottish minister and his battle with kidney failure. Fraser Tallach's brother John wrote in the book's introduction, 'As I thought about God's care over those whose experiences are told in this book it occurred to me that the grace of God, though given in a way which is intimately personal, is not a private matter. Rather it is a public statement about himself which God makes to the world, through the lives of those to whom this grace is given.'

In the words of the hymn 'How Firm a Foundation', God says,

> For I will be with thee, thy troubles to bless,
> And sanctify to thee thy deepest distress.

God doesn't promise to take away our troubles, but he promises to bless them. Elizabeth Goudge, in *The Rosemary Tree*, describes the thoughts of an aged woman crippled by arthritis: 'Pain accepted was just pain, and heavy, but Harriet believed that pain gladly accepted took wings, went somewhere and did something.' For Christians, pain is productive. It takes wings, goes somewhere, and does something. It glorifies God. It sanctifies us. It blesses others. It is with these thoughts in mind that I write about some of the lessons that I learned in the valley.

I learned more about God

Dr Hudson Taylor Armerding, former president of Wheaton College, and Covenant Seminary trustee, suffered from non-Hodgkins lymphoma. We talked when we met at the seminary board meetings, and we exchanged letters and phone calls. I wanted to hear from Dr Armerding about his experience with the same kind of cancer that I had. He would talk with me about it, but not for long. His comments about cancer had a way of turning into words about God. I did not learn all that much about lymphoma from Dr Armerding, but I learned something vastly more important. I learned more about God.

I learned to treasure 'the core doctrines' of the Bible

In Philippians 4:8, 9, the apostle Paul instructs Christians to think about 'whatever is true, whatever is noble, whatever is right, whatever is pure.' Timothy Keller explains that Paul was 'not referring to general loftiness of mind but rather to the specific teaching of the Bible about God, sin, Christ, salvation, the world, human nature, and God's plans for the world – the plan of salvation … Paul is saying if you want peace, think hard and long about the core doctrines of the Bible.'[5] Adolphe Monod's twenty-third Sunday afternoon sermon of his *Farewell*, given in great pain and weakness to friends gathered around his bed, was about the Trinity. This sermon, given just three weeks before he died, follows others on the Bible, Prayer, God, Jesus Christ, and the Holy Spirit.

The Bible furnishes us with a firm foundation that cannot be shaken by sickness and sorrow. I have begun the practice of following my morning reading of the Bible with a chapter of the *Westminster Confession of Faith*. During a sea voyage to Europe, James Henley Thornwell wrote:

> It is now Saturday night, and I must prepare for the holy Sabbath. My Bible and Confession of Faith are my

[5] Keller, *Walking with God*, 298.

travelling companions, and precious friends they have been to me. I bless God for that glorious summary of Christian doctrine contained in our noble standards. It has cheered my soul in many a dark hour, and sustained me in many a desponding moment. I love to read it, and ponder carefully each proof-text as I pass along.[6]

For twenty-five years I taught Calvin's *Institutes of the Christian Religion*, a book in which the French Reformer thinks hard and long about the core doctrines of the Bible. In my book about Calvin's book, I wrote in the preface:

Facing the daily task of living, with its many demands and pressures, struggling with incurable cancer, and trying to find a way to understand the chaos and grimness of world events unfolding around me, I have found Calvin a source of solidity and strength. Enjoying the gift of life, the blessing of love of family and friends, the joy of food and drink, the beauty of nature, and the wonder of it all, I have discovered in Calvin a fellow pilgrim whose words often reflected and focused my feelings and helped me to fix my eyes on heaven and give thanks. Calvin also challenges me, rebukes me, and leads me on, gently but firmly, toward greater love for God and obedience to his word.[7]

[6] Benjamin M. Palmer, *The Life of James Henley Thornwell* (1875; repr. Edinburgh: Banner of Truth Trust, 1975), 162.

[7] David B. Calhoun, *Knowing God and Ourselves: Reading Calvin's Institutes Devotionally* (Edinburgh: Banner of Truth Trust, 2017).

I learned to accept God's plan for my life

When I learned that I had cancer I had many questions. Why was this happening to me? Why was it happening now? Why would God bring into my life something that would hinder and shorten my Christian service? While I was struggling with these things, I read a little book by Southern Baptist preacher Vance Havner, written during the illness and death of his wife, Sara. Havner quoted Matthew 11:6, 'Blessed is the one who is not offended by me' and paraphrased it, 'Blessed is the one who does not get upset by the way I run things.' This, he said, is 'the forgotten beatitude.'[8] I made up my mind to claim that forgotten beatitude. I prayed that I would not be upset by what God was doing with me, but that 'the peace of God, which transcends all understanding' would guard my heart and mind in Christ Jesus (Phil. 4:7).

In the valley I learned the importance of joy, peace, and patience

The 'fruit of the Spirit is love, joy, peace, patience, kindness, goodness, faithfulness, gentleness, self-control' (Gal. 5:22). All Christians need all the fruit of the Spirit all the time, but in the valley I especially needed joy, peace, and patience.

How could I be joyful when my body was slowly, perhaps not so slowly, dying? I have lost sight in one eye and the other eye is failing, as is my hearing. I have been hospitalized seven or eight times in the last three years with

[8] Vance Havner, *Though I Walk Through the Valley* (New York: Revell, 1974). 62-63.

pneumonia. I can no longer swallow food or talk very well. And, most disturbing, my mind is letting me down. How could I be joyful when all this was happening to me? In the valley I learned that joy comes, not from my feelings, nor from my daily experiences, but from the inner conviction that my life is going according to God's plan. Joy is a gift of God. David wrote, 'You have put more joy in my heart than they have when their grain and wine abound' (Psa. 4:7).

In sickness our minds are troubled with a thousand fearful thoughts. We long for peace. Peace, like joy, is a gift of God. Isaiah said to God, 'You keep him in perfect peace whose mind is stayed on you' (Isa. 26:3). In his *Commentary on the Psalms* Calvin wrote that we should pray that God 'would increase our hope when it is small, awaken it when it is dormant, confirm it when it is wavering, strengthen it when it is weak, and that he would even raise it up when it is overthrown. There is no true or solid peace to be enjoyed in the world except in the way of reposing upon the promises of God' (Psa. 51:8). One of the Puritans prayed, 'I have cast my anchor in the port of peace, knowing that [the] present and future are in nail-pierced hands.'[9]

We need joy and peace in the valley. We also need patience – the very word implies suffering. We want our suffering to go away. We want to feel better now. We want things to move quickly. But preaching on Psalm 23:4, Spurgeon told his people that the Christian pilgrim is satisfied to 'walk through the valley of the shadow of death.'

> He does not run in haste: he walks quietly along. We
> are generally in a hurry to get our trouble over … But,

[9] 'Repose,' *The Valley of Vision*.

my dear friend, faith is not in such a frightful bustle – 'He that believeth shall not make haste' (Isa. 28:16). Faith is quick when it has to serve God, but it is patient when it has to wait for him. There is no flurry about the Psalmist, 'Yea, though I walk,' says he – quietly, calmly, steadily. The pace of the experienced man of God is a walk.[10]

Samuel Miller, Princeton Seminary's second professor, loved to tell a story about an old Quaker who met a young man rushing along the road. The young man called out and asked if he could make it to a certain town before nightfall. The Quaker replied, 'Thou mayest get there by sunset if thou goest slow enough.' I have those words (beautifully lettered by my son, Allen) framed and hung where I can see them many times a day. They remind me to be patient.

J. C. Ryle wrote, 'The highest degree of faith is to be able to wait, sit still, and not complain … Jesus loves to show the world that his people can wait.'[11] In *Ash Wednesday*, T. S. Eliot wrote:

> Teach us to care and not to care
> Teach us to sit still.

Psalm 46:10 says, 'Be still, and know that I am God.' In the Psalter of *The Book of Common Prayer*, Psalm 71:14 reads, 'I shall always wait in patience, and shall praise you more and more.'

---

[10] Spurgeon, *Metropolitan Tabernacle Pulpit*, 27:235.
[11] J. C. Ryle, *Power and Sympathy of Christ*, 5, 49.

I learned to walk by faith and not by sight

'The Lord,' Martin Luther said, 'is with me, but not bodily so that I might see or hear him. This presence of the Lord of which I am speaking is not to be grasped by the five senses. But faith sees it and believes surely the Lord is nearer to us than we are to ourselves.'[12] A Puritan prayed, 'Let not faith cease from seeking thee until it vanishes into sight' – which will happen in heaven.[13]

J. C. Ryle wrote, 'The Christian who ... has learned to say, "I believe, and by and by I shall see," has reached a high degree in the school of Christ.'[14] In prison John Bunyan determined, as he put it, 'to live upon God that is invisible' (2 Cor. 4:18). From this conviction was born one of the most beloved Christian books of all time.

Henry Alford wrote:

> We walk by faith, and not by sight;
> > No gracious words we hear
> From him who spoke as none e'er spoke;
> > But we believe him near.
> We may not touch his hands and side,
> > Nor follow where he trod,
> But in his promise we rejoice;
> > And cry, 'My Lord and God!'

In the valley I learned to pray better

Calvin writes that the psalms are 'an anatomy of all parts of the soul ... griefs, sorrows, fears, doubts, hopes, cares,

---

[12] *Luther's Works*, 12:169.
[13] 'A Disciple's Renewal,' *Valley of Vision*.
[14] J. C. Ryle, *Power and Sympathy of Christ*, 84.

perplexities.' The psalms give us prayers for times of deep depression, troubling questions, fearful prospects, failing strength, and fear of death.

Kathleen Norris describes the harrowing experience of trying to care for her husband as he struggled with depression in a North Dakota hospital. A friend phoned and asked her, 'How about you? Are you seeing a doctor? Do you have something to take for this?' Kathleen answered, 'I have the Psalms.' She read and loved the Psalms – all one hundred and fifty of them.[15]

It was not until I entered the valley of the shadow of death that I learned to love and pray the Psalms, all of them. I often pray, 'Help, Lord.' At times that is all I can say, but it is a good prayer, and God hears it. I pray, 'LORD, remember David, and all his afflictions' (Psa. 132:1 KJV). I pray, 'I am yours; save me' (Psa. 119:94). I pray, 'Give ear, O Shepherd of Israel ... stir up your might and come to save us!' (Psa. 80:1, 2).

At other times I pour out my troubles to the Lord and beg him to do something about them. 'When he was in the cave,' David prayed, 'With my voice I cry out to the LORD; with my voice I plead for mercy to the LORD. I pour out my complaint before him; I tell my trouble before him' (Psa. 142:1, 2). In his *Lectures on the Book of Job*, seventeenth-century Scottish preacher James Durham said, 'When straits are straitening ... it is better complaining to God than of God to any other.'[16]

---

[15] Kathleen Norris, *Acedia & Me: A Marriage, Monks, and a Writer's Life* (New York: Riverhead Books, 2008), 77, 276.

[16] James Durham, *Lectures on the Book of Job*, 32.

Many of the Psalms are cries of lament, but these are cries to God, and somewhere in them there are words of hope. Psalm 88 is sometimes called the only lament that has no hope. It ends with the word 'darkness,' but it begins 'O Lord, God of my salvation.' 'We all need to know of this Psalm,' says Fleming Rutledge; 'It teaches us that we can still pray even when we can't pray. No matter how dark and terrible your thoughts may be you can still offer them to God.'[17] The last words of Psalm 88 can be translated 'darkness has become my only companion,' as noted in the English Standard Version. Peter Kreeft quotes 'the unforgettable line of Corrie ten Boom from the depths of a Nazi death camp, "No matter how deep our darkness, he is deeper still."'[18] God is in our darkness. And in his own time and in his own way he will change the night into day. Psalm 88 ends in darkness and despair, but Psalm 89 begins with dazzling light and great joy: 'I will sing of the steadfast love of the Lord forever' (Psa. 89:1).

The prayers of the Psalms are full of pleas and laments, but also full of praise, hope, and trust in God. Eugene Peterson writes that 'most Psalms are complaints. They are calls for help by helpless and hurting men and women ... Our prayers are going to end in praise, but that is going to take a while. Don't rush it. It may take years, decades even, before certain prayers end at hallelujahs.'[19]

---

[17] Rutledge, *The Undoing of Death*, 150.
[18] Quoted by Peter Kreeft, 'Shared Hells,' *Bread and Wine: Readings for Lent and Easter* (New York: Orbis, 2005), 159.
[19] Quoted by Billings, *Rejoicing in Lament*, 173.

In the valley I learned that there are no unanswered prayers.

'The LORD has heard my plea; the LORD accepts my prayer' (Psa. 6:9). Spurgeon writes, '"The LORD will receive my prayer." He will accept it, think of it, and grant it in the way and time which his loving wisdom judges to be best.'[20]

In the *Confessions* Augustine writes that his mother prayed earnestly with many tears that God would not allow him to sail for Rome. She believed that this would be a further and perhaps final step away from the Christian faith. Augustine describes how he set out secretly one night to sail for Rome while his mother was praying and weeping that he not go: 'By her flood of tears what was she begging of you, my God, but that you would not allow me to sail? Yet in your deep counsel you heard the central point of her longing, though not granting her what she then asked, namely that you would make me what she continually prayed for.'[21] Augustine went to Rome and from Rome to Milan, where Monica's deepest prayer was abundantly answered when he came under the influence of Ambrose and was soundly converted to true Christianity.

Timothy Keller writes about praying earnestly, desperately, for an entire year for something he really wanted. He did not get what he asked for. Looking back, Keller says, it was as if God was saying, 'Son, when a child of mine makes a request, I always give that person what he or she would have asked for if they knew everything I know.'[22] Madeleine L'Engle tells about the cancer that took her husband's life,

---

[20] Spurgeon, 'June 6,' *Cheque Book of the Bank of Faith.*

[21] Augustine, *Confessions*, 5.8

[22] Keller, *Walking with God*, 302.

'God comes where there is pain and brokenness, waiting to heal, even if the healing is not the physical one we hope for.'[23] God's healing may not be a temporary one we pray for but the permanent healing of heaven that we long for.

Patrick Miller writes, 'The sound one hears at the end is not the lonely tears of the suffering human being but the music of praise.'[24] The book of Psalms and all our prayers will end the same way – 'Praise the Lord' (Psa. 150:6). One of the Puritans prayed: 'Help me, defend me, until from praying ground I pass to the realm of unceasing praise.'[25]

I learned that time in the valley is not wasted

C. S. Lewis wrote, 'What we regard as a mere hideous interruption and curtailment of life is really the data, the concrete situation on which life is to be built … This at least is what I see at moments of insight; but is hard to remember all the time.'[26]

Charles Haddon Spurgeon said:

> I am sure that I have run more swiftly with a lame leg than I ever did with a sound one. I am certain that I have seen more in the dark than I ever saw in the light – more stars, most certainly – more things in heaven if fewer things on earth. The anvil, the fire,

[23] Madeleine L'Engle, *Two Part Invention: The Story of a Marriage*, (Crosswick Journal) (New York: Farrar Straus & Giroux, 1988), 124.

[24] Miller, *Interpreting the Psalms*, 93.

[25] 'Meeting God,' *The Valley of Vision*.

[26] C. S. Lewis, *They Stand Together: The Letters of C. S. Lewis to Arthur Greeves* (1914–1963), ed. Walter Hooper (London: Collins, 1979), 396, 499.

and the hammer, are the making of us; we do not get fashioned much by anything else. That heavy hammer falling on us helps to shape us; therefore, let affliction and trouble and trial come.[27]

Abraham Kuyper wrote:

A year of your life can never be understood by itself. Every year of your life must be viewed in connection with your whole life here, and with your whole life in the hereafter, because it stands so, and not otherwise, before God, and is so, and not otherwise to be explained ... But if this year [the child of God] must go through a period when God puts him in the smelting furnace, or makes finer cuttings on the diamond of his soul, then, though tears make his eyes glisten, he will nobly bear up in the exaltation of faith; for then it is certain that he is in need of this, that it cannot be otherwise, and that, if it did go otherwise, his life would be a failure forever.[28]

Jesus, who prayed 'Father save me from this hour,' was willing to suffer and die on the cross for all our sins. 'For this purpose I have come to this hour,' Jesus said (John 12:27). To die was the reason God sent Jesus into the world (John 3:16). It was for this purpose that he came.

I must endure the fragility and feelings of uselessness of old age and the destructive effects of cancer and its treatment. It was for this purpose – at least in part – that God sent me into the world. With the psalmist, I 'cry out to God

[27] Quoted by Zack Eswine, *Spurgeon's Sorrows* (Fearn: Christian Focus, 2015), 138..

[28] Abraham Kuyper, *To Be Near Unto God*. tr. John Hendrik de Vries (Grand Rapids: Baker Book House, 1979), 371, 373.

Most High, to God who fulfils his purpose for me' (Psa. 57:2). One of the prayers in *The Valley of Vision* is 'Let me know that the work of prayer is to bring my will to thine.'[29]

'Rejoice in hope, be patient in tribulation, be constant in prayer' (Rom. 12:12)

Much of what I have learned, and am still learning, in the valley of the shadow of death is summed up by the apostle Paul in Romans 12:12 – Don't give up, wait for God, and keep on praying. I know that what I learned in the valley can be lost for a few minutes or a day or even longer. I need to pray every day that the one who is the 'founder' and 'perfecter' of my faith will keep me from 'stumbling' and 'sustain' me to the end (Heb. 12:2; Jude 24; 1 Cor. 1:8). Yesterday, May 29, our fifty-eighth wedding anniversary, Anne and I both prayed from *Daily Prayers*: 'Sustain me, by your strong arm, as I walk in the mists and darkness of the valley, and may I know that your goodness and mercy follow me.'

---

[29] 'Living By Prayer,' *The Valley of Vision*.

EIGHT

YOU PREPARE A TABLE BEFORE ME, IN THE PRESENCE OF MY ENEMIES; YOU ANOINT MY HEAD WITH OIL; MY CUP OVERFLOWS.

JAMES MONTGOMERY
1825

Shepherd of souls, refresh and bless
  Your chosen pilgrim flock
With manna in the wilderness,
  With water from the rock.

Hungry and thirsty, faint and weak,
  As you when here below,
Our souls the joys celestial seek
  Which from your sorrows flow.

We would not live by bread alone,
  But by that word of grace,
In strength of which we travel on
  To our abiding place.

Be known to us in breaking bread,
  But do not then depart;

> Saviour, abide with us, and spread
>> Your table in our heart.
>
> There sup with us in love divine;
>> Your body and your blood,
> That living bread, that heav'nly wine,
>> Be our immortal food.

JAMES MONTGOMERY said about his hymns: 'I lie in wait for my heart and when I can string it to the pitch of David's lyre, I will set a psalm "to the Chief Musician."'[1]

COMMENTARY

G. Campbell Morgan sums up the first five verses of Psalm 23:

> All the circumstances of the pilgrimage – want, weariness, journeyings, wanderings, perplexities, the shadowed mysteries of the valleys, the thronging enemies, and the infinite beyond – are present; and the singer knows them. They are, however, only mentioned to sing of their negation by the graciousness of the Shepherd. Want is cancelled. For weariness he has green pastures of rest. On journeys he leads by pleasant ways. From wanderings he restores. Through perplexities he guides, and that by right ways. In the valleys of death's shadow his presence cancels fear. In the presence of enemies he makes a feast, and he is a host royal in bounty.[2]

---

[1] Cook, *Our Hymn Writers and Their Hymns*, 251.
[2] G. Campbell Morgan, *Notes on the Psalms* (New York: Revell, 1947), 48-49.

The shepherd who leads the sheep to green pastures and quiet waters (verses 1-3) and goes with them into the valley of the shadow of death (verse 4) becomes in verse 5 a kind and generous host, who welcomes his friends to a feast he has lovingly prepared for them. Some writers attempt to continue the shepherd-sheep image of the first four verses of Psalm 23 to verse 5, but it does not fit well.

Those who read and believe the whole Bible know that the Shepherd of the first four verses of Psalm 23 is the Lord Jesus Christ and that the Friend of verse five is the Lord Jesus Christ. John Newton lists ten titles for the Lord in his hymn 'How Sweet the Name of Jesus Sounds':

> Jesus, my Shepherd, Brother, Friend,
> My Prophet, Priest, and King,
> My Lord, my Life, my Way, my End,
> Accept the praise I bring.

Most commentaries use the word 'host' to describe the Lord in verse 5, but some call him 'friend,' including Derek Kidner who writes that the shepherd imagery gives way to one of 'greater intimacy' – that of friend.[3]

You prepare a table before me

David may be remembering the bountiful meal that friends prepared for him when he was fleeing from his enemies – 'wheat, barley, flour, parched grain, beans and lentils, honey and curds and sheep and cheese' (2 Sam. 17:28, 29). God, our friend, David says in Psalm 23:5, prepares a table for us and welcomes us to his feast.

---

[3] Kidner, *Psalms 1–72*, 111.

It is wonderful to be a sheep and look to the Lord as our shepherd. It is awesome (in the old sense of the word) having God as our friend, a friend who invites us to eat and to hold fellowship with him. 'Holy and awesome is his name!' (Psa. 111:9).

We are invited and welcomed to the feast not because of our worthiness but solely because of the graciousness of our host. George Herbert wrote:

> Love bade me welcome: yet my soul drew back,
>   Guilty of dust and sin.
> But quick-ey'd Love, observing me grow slack
>   From my first entrance in,
> Drew nearer to me, sweetly questioning,
>   If I lack'd any thing.
>
> A guest, I answer'd, worthy to be here;
>   Love said, You shall be he.
> I the unkind, ungrateful? Ah my dear,
>   I cannot look on thee.
> Love took my hand, and smiling did reply,
>   Who made the eyes but I?
>
> Truth Lord, but I have marr'd them: let my shame
>   Go where it doth deserve.
> And know you not, says Love, who bore the blame?
>   My dear, then I will serve.
> You must sit down, says Love, and taste my meat:
>   So I did sit and eat.

'Our duty,' wrote the Puritan Richard Sibbes, 'is to accept of Christ's inviting of us. What will we do for him, if we will not feast with him?'[4]

---

[4] Quoted by Dane C. Ortlund, *Gentle and Lowly* (Wheaton: Crossway, 2019), 117.

In the presence of my enemies

Ellen Charry suggests that one way of understanding these words is to understand that the enemies who appear so often and so threateningly throughout the Psalms are those persons and spirits who battle the saints over 'whether God truly is present, gracious, and powerful.'[5] David wrote in Psalm 3:1, 2, 'O LORD, how many are my foes! Many are rising against me; many are saying of my soul, there is no salvation for him in God.' 'Let your steadfast love come to me, O LORD, your salvation according to your promise; then shall I have an answer for him who taunts me, for I trust in your word' (Psa. 119:41, 42). The marks of God's steadfast love are public and unmistakable. In the presence of my enemies 'he [brings] me to the banqueting house, and his banner over me [is] love' (Song of Sol. 2:4).

> Jesus! what a friend of sinners!
>   Jesus! lover of my soul;
> Friends may fail me, foes assail me,
>   He, my Saviour, makes me whole.
>
> Hallelujah! what a Saviour!
>   Hallelujah! what a Friend!
> Saving, helping, keeping, loving,
>   He is with me to the end.
>   (J. Wilbur Chapman, 1859–1918)

You anoint my head with oil

One of John Bunyan's books has the beautiful title *Come and Welcome to Jesus Christ*. The assurance we have of Jesus Christ's welcome to the table that he has prepared is his

---

[5] Ellen Charry, *Psalms 1–50: Sighs and Songs of Israel*, xxii-xxiii.

anointing our heads with oil. Psalm 45:7 (described as 'a love song' in the superscription) says that 'God, your God, has anointed you with the oil of gladness.' It is not one of his servants who anoints our heads with oil, but the Lord himself. We are welcome to come to Jesus, and, wonder of wonders, it is Jesus himself who welcomes us.

> Come, for the feast is spread,
>   Hark to the call;
> Come to the Living Bread,
>   Offered to all.
> Come to his house of wine,
>   Low on his breast recline,
> All that he has is thine;
>   Come, sinner, come.
>
> (Henry Burton, 1840–1930)

My cup overflows

Jesus, the Good Shepherd, came so that his sheep might 'have life, and have it abundantly'! (John 10:10). Jesus, our Friend, fills our cups so full that they overflow! That is God's way. He is *The Prodigal God.*[6] He does not give us just enough to enable us to get by, but a superabundance to cause us to flourish. 'Whoever believes in me, as the Scripture has said, "Out of his heart will flow rivers of living water"' (John 7:38).

Margaret E. Barber (1866–1929), British missionary to China, wrote:

> There is always something over,
>   When we trust our gracious Lord;

[6] Tittle of a book by Timothy J. Keller (New York: Viking, 2008).

Every cup he fills o'erfloweth.
   His great rivers are all broad.
Nothing narrow, nothing stinted,
   Ever issues from his store;
To his own he gives full measure,
   Running over, evermore.

There is always something over,
   When we, from the Father's hand,
Take our portion with thanksgiving,
   Praising for the path he planned.
Satisfaction, full and deepening,
   Fills the soul, and lights the eye,
When the heart has trusted Jesus
   All its needs to satisfy.[7]

The blessings of Psalm 23:5 ('a table for you') take place during the trials of verse 4 ('the valley of the shadow of death'). Timothy and Kathy Keller write in *The Songs of Jesus*: 'God has a celebration meal with us not after we finally get out of the dark valley but in the middle of it, in the presence of our enemies. He wants us to rejoice in him in the midst of our troubles.'[8] The troubles of verse 4 are temporary; the blessings of verse 5 are permanent. Kidner writes, 'To be God's guest is to be more than an acquaintance, invited for a day. It is to live with him.'[9] The Lord keeps on preparing a table for us and anointing our heads with oil and filling our cups all the days of our lives and in heaven we will sit with him in 'the marriage supper of the Lamb' (Rev. 19:9).

[7] Quoted by Mrs Charles E. Cowman, *Streams in the Desert*, 1:172.
[8] Timothy and Kathy Keller, *The Songs of Jesus* (New York: Viking, 2015), 41.
[9] Kidner, *Psalms 1–72*, 112.

PRAYERS, QUOTATIONS, AND STORIES

I am the door of the sheep … I came that they may
have life and have it abundantly.

(John 10:7, 10)

* * *

'You prepare a table before me in the presence of my
enemies' was a favourite text for Communion services in
London churches during the German bombings in World
War II. It affirms that God is present, gracious, and powerful, even in, and especially in, times of great trouble. The
Lord truly loves us and welcomes us to his table even when
bombs are falling all around us.

* * *

One of the most powerful interpretations of Psalm 23
is that of Leonard Bernstein's 'Chichester Psalms,' in
which Psalm 23 is juxtaposed with Psalm 2. The sense
of peace, assurance, and tranquillity arising out of the
imagery of the shepherd and his flock is re-created
musically as chorus and countertenor or boy soprano
sing the twenty-third Psalm in lyric tones. Suddenly
in the midst of this beautiful, quiet melody there erupt
harsh, rapid, and loud sounds of 'the kings of the
earth' raging and plotting together 'against the LORD
and against his anointed' (Psa. 2:2, 3). Tumult takes
over and everything seems to be lost, but slowly above
the chaos one begins to hear again the voice of a young
boy singing the dominant line (musically and exegeti-
cally) of Psalm 23, 'The LORD is my shepherd; I shall

not want.' Gradually the voices of the powerful rulers sputter out and only the melody of trust is left.[10]

* * *

Do not say, 'I will repay evil'; wait for the LORD, and he will deliver you (Prov. 20:22).

> Fear not, O little flock,
>   The foe who madly seeks your overthrow;
> Dread not his rage and pow'r:
>   What though your courage sometimes faints,
> His seeming triumph o'er God's saints
>   Lasts but a little hour.
>
> Be of good cheer; your cause belongs
>   To him who can avenge your wrongs;
> Leave it to him, our Lord:
>   Though hidden yet from all our eyes,
> He sees the Gideon who shall rise
>   To save us and his word.
>
> As true as God's own word is true,
>   Nor earth nor hell with all their crew
> Against us shall prevail.
>   A jest and byword are they grown;
> God is with us, we are his own;
>   Our vict'ry cannot fail.
>
> Amen, Lord Jesus, grant our pray'r;
>   Great Captain, now your arm make bare,
> Fight for us once again;
>   So shall your saints and martyrs raise

[10] Miller, *Interpreting the Psalms*, 118.

A mighty chorus to your praise,
World without end. Amen.
(Johann Michael Altenburg, 1584–1640)

* * *

A Prayer from *The Valley of Vision*:[11]

I thank thee for the temporal blessings of this world –
the refreshing air,
the light of the sun,
the food that renews strength,
the raiment that clothes,
the dwelling that shelters,
the sleep that gives rest,
the starry canopy of night,
the summer breeze,
the flowers' sweetness,
the music of flowing streams,
the happy endearments of family, kindred, friends.
My cup runs over.

My Testimony

I am a preacher (I began when I was fourteen years old, preaching to prisoners in jail in my hometown). I have served as pastor of churches in South Carolina, the West Indies, Illinois, and St Louis, including a Korean Presbyterian Church, Chinese churches, and an African American Baptist Church. Although I preached hundreds of times, I was almost always nervous. Meeting to pray with others before a service, I sometimes quoted the words of the hymn:

[11] 'Evening Praise,' *Valley of Vision*.

Brethren, we have met to worship
  And adore the Lord our God.
Will you pray with all your power,
  While I try to preach the word?

All is vain unless the Spirit
  Of the Holy One come down.
Brethren, pray, and holy manna
  Will be showered all around.
                    (Attr. to George Askins, d. 1816)

I am a teacher, and have taught at Columbia Bible College (now Columbia International University), Jamaica Bible College (where I was also principal), and Covenant Theological Seminary (where I was Professor of Church History).

I was ordained in the Reformed Presbyterian Church, Evangelical Synod. In 1962 the Bible Presbyterian Church (Columbus Synod) had changed its name to the Evangelical Presbyterian Church and three years later merged with the Reformed Presbyterian Church – a denomination with roots reaching back to the days of the Covenanters of Scotland – and became the Reformed Presbyterian Church, Evangelical Synod. Soon after the Presbyterian Church in America was formed in 1973 I transferred into the new denomination. In 1982, a unique 'Joining and Receiving' brought the RPCES into the PCA.

The *Westminster Confession of Faith* states that 'the purest churches under heaven are subject to both mixture and error.'[12] The Presbyterian Church in America is by no means a perfect church, but it has endeavoured under God

---

[12] *Westminster Confession of Faith*, 25:5.

to remain faithful to the Scriptures, loyal to the Westminster Standards, and committed to world missions.

The Presbyterian Church in America has confessed its own toleration of racial discrimination and its failure to stand with black people in their struggle for civil rights. 'Both we and our fathers have sinned; we have committed iniquity; we have done wickedness' (Psa. 106:6). An African American PCA pastor and friend, Michael Campbell, expressed well what has become the conviction and goal of the denomination: 'Christ has made us black, white, Hispanic, Asian, Caribbean, American, and he has made us one. We are to be about recognizing what Christ has done and living it out.'

In 1985 I wrote to Iain Murray to ask whether the Banner of Truth Trust would publish my Ph.D dissertation on Princeton Seminary and missions. 'What we would be interested in,' Mr Murray replied, 'is a full history of Princeton Seminary from 1812 to 1929 – a spiritual, theological, cultural, missionary, and biographical history.' Guided by these five adjectives, I set out to work on a book, which eventually became two volumes. Volume one, *Princeton Seminary: Faith & Learning, 1812–1868*, was published in 1994, and volume two, *Princeton Seminary: The Majestic Testimony, 1869–1929*, came out in 1996.

The Princeton books were followed by other Banner of Truth publications: *Our Southern Zion: Old Columbia Seminary (1828–1927)*; *Pleading for a Reformation Vision: The Life and Selected Writings of William Childs Robinson (1897–1982)*; *Knowing God and Ourselves: Reading Calvin's Institutes Devotionally*; *In Their Own Words: Testimonies of Martin Luther, John Calvin, John Knox, and John Bunyan*;

and *Swift and Beautiful* – chapters of missionary biography. *Grace Abounding: The Life, Books, and Influence of John Bunyan* was published by Christian Focus. I wrote the histories of three great Presbyterian churches of the South: First Presbyterian Church of Columbia, South Carolina (*The Glory of the Lord Risen Upon It 1795–1995*); Independent Presbyterian Church of Savannah, Georgia (*Splendor of Grace 1755–2005*); and First Presbyterian Church of Augusta, Georgia (*Cloud of Witnesses 1804–2004*).

I have a lovely wife, who is now also my competent caregiver. The Puritan Henry Smith said that a good wife is like a present from heaven with these words on it – 'the gift of God.' Anne is God's gift to me. We have been married for almost sixty years. Our marriage has not been without times of tension and conflict, thankfully lessening as the years go by and we grow in grace. One of Anne's Valentine cards describes our marriage well – 'Some high notes, some low notes, but a wonderful song just the same.'

We have two beautiful children who, with their fine spouses, are walking with the Lord. We have two precious grandchildren who are following in their parents' footsteps. 'I will pour my Spirit upon your offspring … This one will say, "I am the LORD's," another will call on the name of Jacob, and another will write on his hand, "The LORD's," and name himself by the name of Israel' (Isa. 44:3, 5). We join with the psalmist in praying, 'Oh, save your people and bless your [and our] heritage! Be their shepherd and carry them forever' (Psa. 28:9).

We have a comfortable house, books and music, and plenty of time to read and rest. We enjoy looking out our windows at the trees and flowers in the summer and watching the snow fall in the winter. Although I can no longer attend church, through the 'miracle' of online streaming, we join worship services on Sunday, always the highlight of our week.

'The LORD is my chosen portion and my cup; you hold my lot. The lines have fallen for me in pleasant places; indeed, I have a beautiful inheritance' (Psa. 16:5, 6).

NINE

SURELY GOODNESS AND MERCY SHALL FOLLOW ME ALL THE DAYS OF MY LIFE.

ISAAC WATTS

1719

My Shepherd will supply my need;
    Jehovah is his name;
In pastures fresh he makes me feed
    Beside the living stream.

He brings my wandering spirit back
    When I forsake his ways,
And leads me for his mercy's sake,
    In paths of truth and grace.

When I walk through the shades of death,
    Thy presence is my stay;
A word of thy supporting breath
    Drives all my fears away.

Thy hand, in sight of all my foes,
    Doth still my table spread;

My cup with blessings overflows,
   Thine oil anoints my head.

The sure provisions of my God
   Attend me all my days;
O may thine house be mine abode,
   And all my work be praise.

There would I find a settled rest,
   While others go and come –
No more a stranger or a guest,
   But like a child at home.

Isaac Watts in 1719 published his *Psalms of David Imitated in the Language of the New Testament*. A young minister asked an older one what commentary he would recommend on the Psalms. The immediate answer was 'Watts's version of them.'

Commentary

Surely goodness and mercy shall follow me all the days of my life

Although not directly stated in the last verse of Psalm 23, we can again imagine the shepherd and his sheep. The sheep have known the shepherd's care every step of the way. He has led them, he has walked beside them, and he has cared for them day and night.

With the memory of past mercies and the reality of present blessings in his mind, David now looks to the future. What he sees is more 'goodness and mercy.' John Updike's last poem, written a few days before his death, ends with the words:

> ... Surely – *magnificent, that 'surely'* –
> goodness and mercy shall follow me all
> the days of my life, *my life, forever*.[1]

F. B. Meyer said that in God there is 'goodness to supply every want, mercy to forgive every sin; goodness to provide, mercy to pardon.'[2] Matthew Henry pictured 'all the streams of mercy flowing from the fountain: pardoning mercy, protecting mercy, sustaining mercy, supplying mercy.'[3] John Newton sang:

> His love in time past forbids me to think
> He'll leave me at last in trouble to sink;
> Each sweet Ebenezer I have in review
> Confirms his good pleasure to help me
>   quite through.[4]

'Goodness and mercy follow me.' The Hebrew word translated 'follow' can be rendered more forcefully. Goodness and mercy pursue us, haunt our steps, they will not let us out of their sight. We are chased, so to speak, not by enemies but by the goodness and mercy of God. The Reformer Martin Bucer wrote, 'People pursue happiness, but happiness pursues the saints and those who entrust themselves to God himself.'[5]

---

[1] John Updike, *Endpoint and Other Poems* (London: Hamish Hamilton, 2009).

[2] Meyer, *The Shepherd Psalm*, 166.

[3] Henry, *Commentary*, 3:259.

[4] From the hymn 'Begone Unbelief! My Saviour Is Near.'

[5] Herman J. Selderhuis ed., *Reformation Commentary on Scripture*, vol. 7: *Psalms 1–72,* (Downers Grove, IL: InterVarsity, 2015), p. 193

God's 'goodness and mercy' will not always appear in forms we expect. C. S. Lewis wrote in *The Problem of Pain*, 'If God is wiser than we [are] his judgment must differ from ours on many things, and not least on good and evil. What seems to us good may therefore not be good in his eyes, and what seems to us evil may not be evil.'[6] Sometimes God says 'no' to the 'good' things we want because they are not really good. And what we call 'bad,' things like cancer, however hurtful and distressing they are to us, are gifts from the Lord who never gives his children a serpent or a scorpion (Luke 11:11, 12). In his last message to his friends gathered around his bed, Adolphe Monod gave thanks to God for his love 'which has afflicted me so much, but has supported me so much.'[7]

A few days before his execution, Dietrich Bonhoeffer wrote:

> And shouldst thou offer us the bitter cup resembling
>   Sorrow, filled to the brim and overflowing,
> We will receive it thankfully, without trembling
>   From thy hand so good and ever-loving.[8]

Patrick Miller writes, 'If you do not have any other verse to carry with you, if you need a way to hold and remember and say all that matters in as simple a form as possible, [here] you have it: "O give thanks to the LORD, for the LORD

---

[6] C. S. Lewis, *The Problem of Pain* (New York: Macmillan Publishing Company, 1962), 37.

[7] Adolphe Monod, tr. Campbell Markham, *Christian Suffering* (Amazon: Kindle, 2017), Farewell Sermon 25.

[8] Bonhoeffer, *My Soul Finds Rest*, 152-53.

is good; God's steadfast love endures forever"[9] God's steadfast love follows me every day of my life. It 'surrounds the one who trusts in the LORD' (Psa. 32:10).

SHEEP AND SHEPHERDS

George Lamsa concluded his book on the Twenty-third Psalm with these words:

> The Lord is my shepherd. He leads us through life, protects us, heals our wounds, meets our needs and feeds us with truth and understanding.
>
> Sheep are symbolical of people who must be led by the prophets and men of God because life is full of difficulties, temptations and sorrows. The desert and the hills are the world where fear, greed and material desires dominate. The migrations are symbolical of the cycles of life. The tents are symbolical of temporal life which is filled with joy, sorrow, prosperity and poverty. One feels sorry to leave this life behind even though it is filled with difficulties.
>
> The homeward journey represents our departure from this life with its struggles into our everlasting home, which is the house of the Lord, where fear, hunger and thirst are unknown. Rivers of living water flow in the green gardens of Paradise, and the Great Shepherd, who never sleeps nor slumbers, stands with staff in his hand and with his wings of protection spread over all.[10]

* * *

[9] Patrick D. Miller, *The Lord of the Psalms* (Philadelphia: Westminster John Knox, 2013), 84.

[10] Lamsa, *The Shepherd of All*, 55.

Douglas MacMillan said:

I remember listening to an old Highland shepherd, an elder, preaching on Psalm 23:6. He was only an old shepherd, not a fancy theologian, but he was wonderful. He said, 'What do I think of when I think of goodness and mercy? I think of the fellows taking the sheep home, walking down the road there with their sticks. The sheep are coming behind them, and behind the sheep are the two dogs, and one is called Goodness and the other is called Mercy … Ah! They are two lovely dogs, Goodness and Mercy.' I think if I was still shepherding, and I still had two dogs, I would call one Goodness and I would call the other Mercy, because it is a very true picture.[11]

Prayers, Quotations, and Stories

Listen to me, O house of Jacob, all the remnant of the house of Israel, who have been borne by me from before your birth, carried from the womb, even to your old age I am he, and to gray hairs I will carry you. I have made, and I will bear; I will carry and will save.

(Isa. 46:3, 4)

* * *

'If you are the Lord's sheep,' said C. H. Spurgeon, 'you shall be protected, provided for, and guided till you reach the upper fold on the hilltop of glory.'[12]

* * *

[11] MacMillan, *The Lord Our Shepherd*, 82.
[12] Spurgeon, *Metropolitan Tabernacle Pulpit*, 52:462.

Susannah Spurgeon described her life with her husband as 'two pilgrims treading this highway of life together, hand in hand – heart linked to heart.' Their journey, she wrote, was one of mostly 'singing,' but eventually 'they came to a place on the road where two ways met; and here, amidst the terrors of a storm such as they had never before encountered, they parted company.' But the 'goodness and mercy which for many years had followed the two travellers, did not leave the solitary one,' but rather the Lord 'led on softly, and chose green pastures for the tired feet, and still waters for the solace and refreshment of his trembling child.'[13]

* * *

Newsweek (for August 14, 2006) featured a picture of Billy Graham on its cover and an eight-page article about the then eighty-seven-year-old evangelist. It began:

> Earlier this summer, on a warm Carolina evening, Billy Graham awoke in the middle of the night … He lay in the darkness, trying to recite the 23rd Psalm from memory. He begins: 'The LORD is my shepherd, I shall not want.' Then, for a moment, he loses the thread, but soon the last line comes back to him: 'Surely goodness and mercy shall follow me all the days of my life; and I shall dwell in the house of the Lord forever.' Relieved, he drifts back to sleep.

* * *

[13] Ray Rhodes Jr., *Susie: The Life and Legacy of Susannah Spurgeon, wife of Charles H. Spurgeon* (Chicago: Moody Publishers, 2018), 220.

John McDuff wrote that David loved to sit at the

> windows of covenant faithfulness, looking, at one
> time, back along the checkered vista behind him, and
> then casting a glance across the river of death into the
> shining city. 'Goodness and Mercy,' the two attendant
> guardian angels that have tracked his footsteps all the
> bygone way, he sees still at his side. Other messengers
> … have met him on the road. Sorrow, clad in her
> sombre attire; Bereavement, with her tearful eye;
> Pain, with her languid countenance. But his joyful,
> contented spirit can see none in all the train save two
> – Goodness and Mercy![14]

My Testimony

Both my parents – faithful Christians who raised me
and my two brothers in the 'fear and admonition of the
Lord' – lived long, productive lives. Toward the end of
his life my father wrote what he called his 'testimony.' He
ended it with the words, 'I am now ninety-two years old
and continue to preach occasionally and to give testimony
to the Lord's faithfulness. My main interest is in the coming
of the Lord. I trust that you are ready.' He died a few years
later, expressing his desire 'to go home.'

In his testimony my father wrote about my mother. 'My
wife, Pauline, who is from the mountains of Kentucky, and
is one of the sincerest Christians I have ever known, was
a wonderful source of strength and encouragement. She

[14] John McDuff, *The Shepherd and His Flock; or, The Keeper of
Israel and the Sheep of His Pasture* (New York: Robert Carter &
Brothers, 1866), 108.

brought our little children – David, Paul, and John – and spent every Sunday with me at the church I had begun in the country.' My father was a pharmacist, and my mother worked in his drugstore and also helped him with his sermons (although only a high school graduate, she was a better Bible student than he was). She took care of her three boys, and found time to teach Bible in the Sumter County schools, black and white, as well as at the 'Turk' school for children who were thought to be descendants of the Turkish servants of the Revolutionary War General Thomas Sumter.

All her life, and right up to the end, my mother looked forward to Sunday, when, as a Southern lady, she put on her best dress and hat, and went to church, morning and evening. The last years of her life she lived with my brother and his wife. In that house there were four generations, separated by a hundred years in age but united in love. My mother was always happy and cheerful. I prayed that God would give her a good ending to her long life, and he did. She died in December 2017. She was ninety-nine years old. Her last words were 'I'm waiting,' and then God took her to her heavenly home. 'Those who wait for me shall not be put to shame' (Isa. 49:23).

My brother Paul died as a young man. When he was a boy he had surgery for a non-malignant mass in his brain. He survived the surgery but lived with its debilitating effects the rest of his short life. As he became weaker in body, he grew stronger in faith. We saw God's goodness and mercy in both his life and his death. He told me one day, 'I want to be a butterfly, something beautiful that can go places without a wheelchair.' Paul got his wish. He is now completely free from the limitations and hardships of his earthly life, and someday his body will be raised from the dead, a body more beautiful than any butterfly, and more glorious than he ever imagined.

Six months after my mother died, my brother John suddenly died. For years he had struggled with heart problems, but he seemed to be feeling well. One afternoon he lay down to rest, went to sleep, and woke up in heaven. Surely God's goodness and mercy followed him to the very end.

Over thirty years ago I was diagnosed with an incurable cancer. I know that it came to me from God, as did the apostle Paul's 'thorn in the flesh.' Three times Paul pled with the Lord that he would be free of it. God did not take away the apostle's 'thorn,' but he did something better. God gave him the promise: 'My grace is sufficient for you, for my power is made perfect in weakness' (2 Cor. 12:9). God's power was present in the days of the apostle Paul's strength, but it was 'made perfect' in his weakness. In my long struggle with cancer, I have experienced one debilitating problem after another. Cancer and sickness have followed me, pursued me, haunted me for the last thirty years. I have been hospitalized many times. But all these 'thorns' are really blessings in disguise. I am sure of it, and in heaven I shall be doubly sure. Writing about Psalm 23 Artur Weiser quotes these lines from a German hymn:

> Could I from on high in heaven
>   Once my former life survey,
> Then I'd in stirring measure say,
>   'Thou hast led and blessed my way.'[15]

[15] Weiser, *The Pslams*, 229.

On many of the Sundays of my life, I have been in the pulpit of a church to preach the word of God. I preached my last sermon over five years ago. Since then I have been unable to preach because of my many health problems. And I miss it! In May 1916 Alexander Whyte (1836–1921) wrote to the congregation of St George's United Free Church to say that he was resigning as pastor because of his 'decaying strength.' Whyte was not looking forward to his 'silent Sabbaths' to come, he said, but he found an encouraging example in Thomas Boston, who 'came to see ... that some years of silent Sabbaths are a good way of winding up a pulpit and pastoral life, and a good opportunity of making preparation for the better life and better services in the Upper Sanctuary.'[16]

Surely, goodness and mercy have followed me all the days of my life. I pray, with George Herbert, 'Thou that hast given so much to me; give one more thing, a grateful heart.'[17]

[16] Quoted in Michael A. G. Haykinn, *A Consuming Fire: The Piety of Alexander Whyte* (Grand Rapids: Reformation Heritage Books, 2006), 118.

[17] George Herbert, *The Works of George Herbert* ed. F. E. Hutchinson (Oxford: Clarendon Press, 1941), 123.

CHAPTER TEN

AND I SHALL DWELL IN THE HOUSE OF THE LORD FOREVER.

REFORMATION HYMN

1531

The Lord is my faithful shepherd,
He holds me in his protection,
Where there is nothing lacking to me
At all of any goodness.
He puts me out to pasture continually
Where grows the sweet-tasting grass
   Of his holy word.

He leads me to pure water
That brings me refreshment.
It is his Holy Spirit
That makes me cheerful.
He guides me on the right road
Of his commandments without ceasing
   On account of his name's sake.

And though I wander in the dark valley,
I fear no misfortune

In persecution, suffering, sorrow
And the spiteful malice of this world,
For you are with me constantly.
Your rod and staff comfort me.
   I rely on your word.

You prepare for me a table
Before my enemies on all sides.
You make my heart undismayed and fresh.
You anoint my head for me,
With your Spirit, the oil of joy,
And you pour out fully in my soul
   Your spiritual joy.

Goodness and mercy
Follow me through my life,
And I shall remain forever
In the house of the Lord,
On earth in Christian company
And after death I shall be there
   With Christ my Lord.

In his commentary on the Psalms, Artur Weiser quoted this hymn from the German Reformation and wrote that it is 'entirely in accordance with the keynote of Psalm 23 when the Reformation hymn … supplements at its conclusion the idea of communion on earth by the idea of communion with Christ after death.'[1]

[1] Weiser, *The Psalms*, 231, f.2.

COMMENTARY

And I shall dwell in the house of the Lord forever

The sheepfold of verses 1-4 of the Twenty-third Psalm and the banqueting table of verse 5 become, in verse 6, the 'house of the LORD.' How suggestive and significant is that little word 'and' in the middle of the psalm's last line – 'Surely goodness and mercy shall follow me all the days of my life, *and* I shall dwell in the house of the LORD forever.' F. Crossley Morgan wrote: 'One is inclined to say to David, "But surely you have reached the end, you have spoken of all the days of your life." Ah no! not the end but the beginning! The great commencement! The great graduation!'[2]

The last word of Psalm 23, translated 'forever' in the KJV and the ESV, is literally 'for length of days' in the Hebrew. The note in the *ESV Study Bible* acknowledges the possibility that the word means 'all the days of my life,' but states that it is more likely to mean 'for days without end,' that is, *forever*. Derek Kidner writes that 'length of days' is not an expression for eternity, 'but since the logic of God's covenant allows no ending to his commitment to a man, as our Lord pointed out [in Matt. 22:31, 32], the Christian understanding of these words does no violence to them.'[3] Dietrich Bonhoeffer wrote, 'The Psalms request fellowship with God in earthly life, but they know that this fellowship is not completed in earthly life but continues beyond it.'[4] William Plumer said that the last words of the psalm point

[2] Morgan, *A Psalm of an Old Shepherd*, 62.

[3] Kidner, *Psalms 1–72*, 130.

[4] Bonhoeffer, *The Prayer Book of the Bible*, 61-62.

'not only to great blessings arising from communion with God on earth; but to still higher, richer enjoyments of those who worship in the sanctuary above.'[5] Bruce Waltke states that 'all the days of my life' refer to the psalmist's earthly life, 'but that is not the climactic end of the drama' of Psalm 23, as the rest of verse 6 makes clear, '"and I shall dwell in the house of the LORD forever."'[6] J. Todd Billings says that 'God's repeated promise that "I will be their God and they will be my people" needs to overcome death in order to have its ultimate fulfilment.'[7]

SHEEP AND SHEPHERDS

On a rainy, windy day my son Allen and I were walking on the northern part of the Isle of Lewis in the Outer Hebrides of Scotland. We came upon an old shepherd and his sheep. In that remote place we had not seen anyone else all day. The shepherd had a quiet calmness about him. He knew what he was doing. He knew his sheep and they knew him. He knew the boggy, deceptive, dangerous terrain. He had been over that ground many times. He led his sheep safely along the solid path, which we had trouble finding without many missteps. He steered his sheep away from the cliffs that fell away to the rocks far below and the pounding surf of the Atlantic. The sheep stayed close to the shepherd, a few in front and the rest following, and when the safe path was wider they surrounded him. The sheep appeared to be content, even happy. Not at all like a solitary sheep we had

[5] Plumer, *Psalms*, 316.
[6] Waltke & Houston, *The Psalms as Christian Worship*, 444.
[7] Billings, *Rejoicing in Lament*, 12.

seen earlier, alone with no shepherd in sight, calling out in distress.

The wind blew harder and the rain pelted down as Allen and I watched the shepherd and his sheep. With a twinkle in his eye, he greeted us with the words 'A fine day.' I wondered, was it a joke or is that what Scots always say, regardless of the weather? I think the old shepherd meant it. The skies were dark and the wind sharp, but you can't judge a day by its weather! The shepherd was happy to be a shepherd. He was glad that his sheep were safely with him. They did not appear to be in a hurry, but before long they were out of sight. They were on their way home, which meant for the sheep a cosy shelter in the shepherd's house, and for the shepherd a warm peat fire and singing tea kettle. Yes, it was a fine day.

PRAYERS, QUOTATIONS, AND STORIES

They shall hunger no more, neither thirst anymore; the sun shall not strike them, nor any scorching heat. For the Lamb in the midst of the throne will be their Shepherd, and he will guide them to springs of living water; and God will wipe away every tear from their eyes.

(Rev. 7:16, 17)

* * *

Douglas MacMillan wrote:

In Psalm 22 you find a depiction of the Good Shepherd [John 10:11] laying down his life for the sheep. In Psalm 23 you find the Great Shepherd [Heb. 13:20] who has taken his life again, and who lovingly will shepherd and pastor every one of his sheep and lead them ... to the Father's house for evermore. And then in Psalm 24 you have the glory of the Chief Shepherd [1 Pet 4:12], the one who is ascended into glory in order to give glory to his sheep, to make them like himself. I once heard Professor Finlayson preaching on Psalm 23, and he linked Psalm 22 to Psalm 24 like this: 'One is the psalm of the cross, the next is the psalm of the crook, and the third is the psalm of the crown.' They stand together, and each of them sheds its own particular light upon the Shepherd who is our Shepherd, our Lord Jesus Christ. And these lights blend, and they light up his glory, and they show him to be a Great Shepherd.

There is a verse which I think sums up all I have been trying to say in relation to Psalms 22, 23 and 24. It is this: 'The LORD is a sun and shield: the LORD will give grace and glory; no good thing will he withhold from them that walk uprightly' (Psa. 84:11). 'The LORD will give grace' – he has done that; that is what Psalm 22 is all about. And then 'the LORD will give glory' – Psalm 24 ... And what is in between? Psalm 23. He gives grace and he gives glory, and in between these two it is true that 'he will withhold no good thing from them that walk uprightly.' That is what Psalm 23 is about. It is about the Shepherd's giving of every blessing that the sheep will ever need.[8]

* * *

---

[8] MacMillan, *The Lord Our Shepherd*, 20-21, 42.

M. P. Krikorian wrote:

> For me the most cherished hour of the day, as a shepherd, was the early evening when the high hills and stately trees cast their kindly shadows across the face of the fields in holy solemnity. I knew then that it was time to go home. The sheep also instinctively seem to sense the significance of these signs. At the sound of the pipe or an evensong of soft melody by the shepherd, they literally and with great charm dance onward in their happy journey homeward, a few picking up here and there the last mouthful of food ere they enter the fold. So are the true sons of God, children of the heavenly king, who rejoice at the happy prospect of being in the fold permanently with their Shepherd Lord, singing on their joyous journey homeward, 'O that will be ... glory for me.'[9]

* * *

> We give thee hearty thanks, for that it hath pleased thee to deliver this our brother/sister out of the miseries of this sinful world; beseeching thee that it may please thee of thy gracious goodness, shortly to accomplish the number of thine elect, and to hasten thy kingdom, that we, with all those that are departed in the true faith of thy holy Name, may have our perfect consummation and bliss, both in body and soul, in thy eternal and everlasting glory, through Jesus Christ our Lord. Amen.[10]

* * *

[9] Krikorian, *The Spirit of the Shepherd*, 154.

[10] A prayer from the Service for the burial of the dead, *Book of Common Prayer*.

When I was in high school someone gave me a little book by C. H. Spurgeon, *The Check Book of the Bank of Faith*. I have quoted it often in this book. Spurgeon presents a promise of the Bible for every day in the year, and urges the reader to cash the cheque, that is, claim the promise. The promise for the last day of the year is Psalm 73:24 – 'Thou shalt guide me with thy counsel, and afterward receive me to glory.' Spurgeon ends with words of testimony:

> Soon the end will come: a few more years, and I must depart out of this world unto the Father. My Lord will be near my bed. He will meet me at heaven's gate: he will welcome me to the glory-land. I shall not be a stranger in heaven: my own God and Father will receive me to its endless bliss.

* * *

Henry Francis Lyte (1793–1847), a Church of England pastor and hymn writer, whispered as he was dying, 'O there is nothing terrible in death. Jesus Christ steps down into the grave before me … Blessed faith! Today piercing through the mist of earth; tomorrow changed to sight.'

* * *

In the hymn 'Guide Me, O Thou Great Jehovah,' William Williams (1717–91) wrote:

> When I tread the verge of Jordan,
> Bid my anxious fears subside;
> Death of death, and hell's destruction,
> Land me safe on Canaan's side;
> Songs of praises
> I will ever give to thee.

My Testimony

'No eye has seen, nor ear heard, nor the heart of man imagined, what God has prepared for those who love him,' – 'these things God has revealed to us through the Spirit' (1 Cor. 2:9, 10). Heaven will be amazing, astounding, over-whelming, but it will not be strange. It will not be like going to a foreign country, where we don't know the language, the customs, or the people. It will be more like coming home after a long (or, for some, not so long) journey in a distant land. Puritan pastor Richard Baxter, who wrote *The Saints' Everlasting Rest*, said that every Christian should think about heaven for half an hour every day. To help me do this I sometimes read again the chapter in Calvin's *Institutes* called 'Meditation on the Future Life.'[11] Heaven is wonderful, but death is terrible. John Calvin wrote: 'Surely it is terrifying to walk in the darkness of death; and believers, whatever their strength may be, cannot but be frightened by it.'[12] 'Death is ugly, a rotted deal; it is a cheat, a thief, a grinning mockery,' writes Fleming Rutledge.[13]

But death's days are numbered. The crucifixion and resurrection of Jesus Christ have defeated death and in God's time that victory will be completed. In 1 Corinthians 15 – the great chapter on the resurrection of Christ and the future resurrection of the dead – the apostle Paul writes (quoting Isa.25:8):

[11] John Calvin, tr. F. L. Battles, *Institutes of the Christian Religion*, (Philadelphia: Westminster John Knox Press, 1960), III.x.

[12] Calvin, *Institutes*, III.ii.21.

[13] Fleming Rutledge, *The Undoing of Death* (Grand Rapids: Eermans, 2005), 276.

> Death is swallowed up in victory.
> O death, where is your victory?
> O death, where is your sting?

John Donne addressed death in famous words:

> Death, be not proud, though some have called thee
> Mighty and dreadful, for thou art not so,
> For those whom thou think'st thou dost overthrow
> Die not, poor Death, nor yet canst thou kill me …
> One short sleep past, we wake eternally,
> And death shall be no more; Death, thou shalt die.[14]

The crucifixion and resurrection of Jesus Christ guarantee the death of death and the 'undoing of death.' Death shall die and all the works of Satan, including death, will be undone. Throughout history the struggle between the seed of the serpent and the seed of the woman (Gen. 3:15) shows the victory of the devil and his hosts over God and his people. But that will be changed suddenly when 'the Lord himself will descend from heaven with a cry of command, with the voice of an archangel, and with the sound of the trumpet of God' (1 Thess. 4:16). His 'cry of command' will herald the final 'undoing of death' and the creation of a new heaven and a new earth, where 'death shall be no more, neither shall there be any mourning nor crying nor pain anymore, for the former things have passed away' (Rev. 21:4). The *Westminster Confession of Faith* states that in Christ we are already free from 'the evil of afflictions, the sting of death, the victory of the grave.'[15] Some day we will be free from all afflictions, from death itself, and from

[14] John Donne, Holy Sonnet No. 10.
[15] *Westminster Confession of Faith*, 20.1.

the grave. 'The inexorability of death has been reversed; its remorselessness has been overcome; its effects have been undone. We see this now by faith; in the Resurrection day we shall see it face to face.'[16]

In one of her short poems, Mary Oliver (1935–2019) writes about death and what comes after it:

> Don't think
> I'm not afraid.
> There is such an unleashing
> Of horror.
> Then I remember:
> Death comes before
> The rolling away
> Of the stone.[17]

On the third day, the stone was rolled away and Jesus rose from the dead. He 'got up,' as my friends in the African American church love to say. He 'lay down in the grave, and rose again for us,' in the language of the *Book of Common Prayer*.[18] In the words of Fleming Rutledge, 'Jesus exploded from the grave.'[19]

When I die my body will die, but I will live on 'in the house of the LORD,' rejoicing in the wonders of heaven and eagerly waiting the day when my earthly body will 'get up,' and I will be a complete person again. In *Hymns from the Land of Luther* we hear a believer speaking to his body:

---

[16] Rutledge, *The Undoing of Death*, 328.

[17] Mary Oliver, *Devotions: Selected Poems* (New York: Penguin Press, 2017), 183.

[18] 'Morning Prayer to be used in Families.'

[19] Rutledge, *Help My Unbelief*, 164.

Go to thy quiet resting,
  Poor tenement of clay!
From all thy pain and weakness
  I gladly haste away;
But still in faith confiding
  To find thee yet again,
All glorious and immortal –
  Good night, till then![20]

When we die, our souls leave our bodies, but Jesus does not leave our bodies. These bodies, still 'united to Christ,' rest in their graves until the resurrection.[21] Jesus said, 'Whoever believes in me, though he die, yet shall he live. Do you believe this?' (John 11:26). Spurgeon answers, 'Yes, Lord, we believe it; we shall never die. Our soul may be separated from our body, and this is death of a kind; but our soul shall never be separated from God, which is the true death.'[22] And some day, our bodies will live again, and be made to be like Christ's glorious body, 'by the power that enables him even to subject all things to himself' (Phil. 3:21).

The resurrection of our bodies is the great ultimate hope, but there is another, more immediate, hope in the words of Jesus to the thief on the cross, 'Truly, I say to you, today you will be with me in Paradise' (Luke 23:43).

The sad last words of Oscar Wilde, it is said, were, 'I am dying beyond my means.' That is true of all of us. But what we cannot do, God has done. 'Truly no man can ransom another, or give to God the price of his life … But God will

[20] Quoted in J. C. Ryle, *Power and Sympathy of Christ* 127.
[21] *Westminster Larger Catechism*, Q. 86.
[22] Spurgeon, 'July 11,' *Cheque Book of the Bank of Faith*.

ransom my soul from the power of Sheol [the grave KJV], for he will receive me' (Psa. 49:7, 15). 'For Christ suffered once for sins, the righteous for the unrighteous, that he might bring us to God' (1 Pet. 3:18). In the words of Thomas Cranmer's prayer for Communion, God is 'not weighing our merits but pardoning our iniquities, through Jesus Christ our Lord.' 'In him ... grace has almost out-graced itself,' one of the Puritans said.[23]

One of Johann Sebastian Bach's cantatas repeats the good news that 'Jesus has died for me, and his death is my profit; he has won for me salvation, therefore I joyfully go from here, away from the bustle of the world into God's beautiful heaven, where I shall forever behold the Trinity.'[24] William Plumer wrote, 'God is the believer's portion. Christ is his elect Saviour. The Holy Spirit is his Comforter.'[25] We can be sure that when we come to the river of death, the triune God who has been with us all the way, will go with us through death itself, when 'all other guides turn back,' and, it seems, 'the traveller must go on alone.'[26]

These words from Calvin are quoted earlier in this chapter, 'Surely it is terrifying to walk in the darkness of death; and believers, whatever their strength may be, cannot but be frightened by it.' That sentence is followed by another, 'But since the thought prevails that they have God beside them, caring for their safety, fear at once yields to assurance.'[27]

[23] 'Love Shed Abroad,' *Valley of Vision*.
[24] *Alle Menschen Mussen Sterben*.
[25] Plumer, *Psalms*, 317.
[26] Kidner, *Psalms 1–72*, 111.
[27] Calvin, *Institutes*, III.ii.21.

The story of my life on earth is not yet over. It may be the last chapter. It may even be the last page. 'It's not your job to tie up the loose ends,' writes J. Todd Billings. 'It's not your job to make sense of everything ... Let God gather up the fragments. Let God finish the story.'[28]

Lord, I pray, finish the story in your own way, and then 'let me go generously, even joyfully, into that "good night" that opens into "resurrection morning."'[29]

---

[28] Billings, *Rejoicing in Lament*, 109.
[29] Marilyne Chandler McEntyre, *A Faithful Farewell: Living Your Last Chapter with Love* (Grand Rapids: Eerdmans, 2015), 139.

BENEDICTION

Now may the God of peace
who brought again from the dead our Lord Jesus,
the great shepherd of the sheep,
by the blood of the eternal covenant,
equip you with everything good
that you may do his will,
working in us that which is pleasing in his sight,
through Jesus Christ,
to whom be glory for ever and ever.
Amen.

HEBREWS 13:20

ADDENDUM

ADDITIONAL VERSIONS OF
PSALM 23

The Lord Is Only My Support
William Whittingham

1556

William Whittingham 'combined scholastic ability, the practical skill of a man of affairs, and the idealism of the Puritan.'[1] Encouraged by Calvin and the example of the French Psalter, Whittingham and other English refugees in Geneva published their own Anglo-Geneva Psalter, *The Form of Prayers and Psalms of David*. For it, Whittingham wrote the first metrical version of Psalm 23 in English.

> The Lord is only my support
> And he that doth me feed:
> How can I then lack anything
> Whereof I stand in need?
>
> In pastures green he feedeth me,
> Where I do safely lie:
> And after leads me to the streams,
> Which run most pleasantly.
>
> And when I find myself near lost,
> Then doth he me home take,
> Conducting me in his right paths,
> E'en for his own name's sake.
>
> And tho' I were e'en at death's door
> Yet would I fear no ill:

[1] Lewis Lupton, *A History of the Geneva Bible*, (London: Fauconberg/Olive Tree, 1966-81) 3:138.

For both thy rod and shepherd's crook,
   Afford me comfort still.

Thou hast my table richly spread
   In presence of my foe;
Thou hast my head with balm refresh'd,
   My cup doth overflow.

The Lord Is My Shepherd
Geneva Bible

1560

When Queen Mary Tudor died, most of the English exiles in Geneva returned home, but William Whittingham stayed on to oversee the completion of the translation of the Geneva Bible. The Geneva Bible, writes Jane Dawson, 'became a bestseller and by far the most popular version for the people of Protestant Scotland, Elizabethan England, and the early American colonies.'[2]

> The Lord is my shepherd, I shall not want.
> He maketh me to rest in green pasture,
>   And leadeth me by the still waters.
> He restoreth my soul,
>   And leadeth me in the paths of righteousness
>   For his Name's sake.
> Yea, though I should walk through the valley
>   Of the shadow of death,
>   I will fear no evil:
> For thou art with me:
>   Thy rod and thy staff, they comfort me.
> Thou dost prepare a table before me,
>   In the sight of my adversaries:
> Thou dost anoint mine head with oil,
>   And my cup runneth over.
> Doubtless kindness and mercy shall follow me,
>   All the days of my life,

[2] Jane Dawson, *John Knox* (Yale, 2017), 153.

And I shall remain a long season
In the house of the LORD.

THE GOD OF LOVE MY SHEPHERD IS
GEORGE HERBERT

1633

Studying at Cambridge George Herbert seemed set for a distinguished public career, but chose instead to be ordained as an priest in the Church of England in 1630. He spent the rest of his short life serving a tiny rural parish in Bemerton near Salisbury. His collection of Christian poems, *The Temple*, first published in 1633, shows his warm, genuine faith, poetic genius, and humble character.

> The God of love my shepherd is,
>   And he that doth me feed;
> While he is mine and I am his,
>   What can I want or need?
>
> He leads me to the tender grass,
>   Where I both feed and rest;
> Then to the streams that gently pass:
>   In both I have the best.
>
> Or if I stray, he doth convert,
>   And bring my mind in frame.
> And all this not for my desert,
>   But for his holy name.
>
> Yea, in death's shady black abode
>   Well may I walk, not fear;
> For thou art with me, and thy rod
>   To guide, thy staff to bear.

Surely thy sweet and wondrous love
  Shall measure all my days;
And as it never shall remove,
  So neither shall my praise.

The Lord To Me A Shepherd Is
Bay Psalm Book

1640

The *Bay Psalm Book*, a metrical version of the Psalms, was the first book to be printed in British America. It is the work of a body of Puritan ministers, among them Richard Mather, father of Increase and grandfather of Cotton Mather, and John Owen, pastor at Roxbury and missionary to the Algonquian Indians.

> The LORD to me a shepherd is,
> Want therefore shall not I.
> He in the folds of tender grass,
> Doth cause me down to lie:
>
> To waters calm me gently leads.
> Restore my soul doth he.
> He doth in paths of righteousness
> For his name's sake lead me.
>
> Yea though in valley of death's shade
> I walk, none ill I'll fear,
> Because thou art with me, thy rod,
> And staff my comfort are.
>
> For me a table thou hast spread,
> In presence of my foes.
> Thou dost anoint my head with oil,
> My cup it overflows.

Goodness and mercy surely shall
　　All my days follow me,
And in the LORD's house I shall dwell
　　So long as days shall be.

Through All My Life

John Bunyan

1684

In Part Two of *The Pilgrim's Progress*, Christiana and her companions spent a happy month in the Porter's Lodge where they rested and received spiritual instruction. As the pilgrims were leaving the lodge, they heard the birds in the grove singing to them from Sternhold's and Hopkins's version of Psalm 23 (an early metrical Psalter).

> Through all my life thy favour is
>   So frankly show'd to me,
> That in thy house for evermore
>   My dwelling-place shall be.
>
> For why? The Lord our God is good,
>   His mercy is for ever sure;
> His truth at all times firmly stood,
>   And shall from age to age endure.

THE LORD MY PASTURE SHALL PREPARE
JOSEPH ADDISON

1712

Son of a minister, Joseph Addison was educated at
Oxford and became an important figure in English politi-
cal and literary history. He was one of the founders of the
Spectator, which attempted to restore good sense and high
standards to a society that suffered from the extremes of
the Restoration. F. W. Boreham writes about how Joseph
Addison as a child learned Psalm 23. 'He learned the words,
innocently and thoughtlessly, at his mother's knee; but they
became the song, the strength, and the solace of his later
life.'[3]

> The Lord my pasture shall prepare
>   And feed me with a shepherd's care;
> His presence shall my wants supply,
>   And guard me with a watchful eye.
> My noonday walks he shall attend,
>   And all my midnight hours defend.
>
> When in the sultry glebe I faint,
>   Or on the thirsty mountains pant,
> To fertile vales and dewey meads
>   My weary, wandering steps he leads
> Where peaceful rivers soft and slow
>   Amid the verdant landscape flow.

[3] Boreham, *In Pastures Green*, ix.

Though in a bare and rugged way
   Through devious, lonely wilds I stray,
Thy bounty shall my paths beguile;
   The barren wilderness shall smile,
With sudden greens and herbage crowned,
   And streams shall murmur all around.

Though in the path of death I tread,
   With gloomy horrors overspread,
My steadfast heart shall fear no ill,
   For thou, O Lord, art with me still;
Thy friendly staff give me aid
   And guide me through the dreadful shade.

WHEN ALL YOUR MERCIES, O MY GOD
JOSEPH ADDISON

1712

Joseph Addison said, 'David has very beautifully represented steady reliance on God Almighty in his twenty-third
psalm.'

> When all your mercies,
>   O my God, my rising soul surveys,
> Transported with the view,
>   I'm lost in wonder, love, and praise.
>
> Unnumbered comforts to my soul
>   Your tender care bestowed,
> Before my infant heart conceived
>   From whom those comforts flow'd.
>
> When worn with sickness,
>   Oft have you with health renewed my face;
> And when in sins and sorrows sunk,
>   Revived my soul with grace.
>
> Ten thousand thousand precious gifts
>   My daily thanks employ;
> Nor is the least a cheerful heart
>   That tastes those gifts with joy.
>
> Through ev'ry period of my life
>   Your goodness I'll pursue;
> And after death, in distant worlds,
>   The glorious theme renew.

When nature fails, and day and night
   Divide thy works no more,
My ever grateful heart, O Lord,
   Thy mercy shall adore.

Through all eternity
   To you a joyful song I'll raise;
For oh, eternity's too short
   To utter all your praise.

Sheep May Safely Graze
Johann Sebastian Bach

1713

Bach wrote 'Sheep May Safely Graze' in 1713 as part of his Cantata No. 208, praising secular rulers who wisely govern and so furnish their people peace and prosperity. Bach's words applied beautifully to God's care for his own, and were made into a short hymn of praise. There are different English translations, including the following, the second of which is commonly used as the text for the hymn.

> Sheep may safely graze and pasture
>   In a watchful shepherd's sight.
> Those who rule, with wisdom guiding,
>   Bring to hearts a peace abiding,
>   Bless a land with joy made bright.
>
> Sheep may safely graze and pasture
>   Where the shepherd guards them well.
> So the nation ruled in wisdom
>   Knows and shares the many blessings
>   Which both peace and plenty bring.

My Shepherd is the Lamb
John Beaumont
1762–1822

Little is known about this English author. His version of Psalm 23 begins by linking the 'Shepherd' of the psalm with 'the Lamb of God, who takes away the sin of the world' (John 1:29). In the book of Revelation Jesus is described as both Shepherd and Lamb. 'For the Lamb in the midst of the throne will be their shepherd, and he will guide them to springs of living water, and God will wipe away every tear from their eyes' (Rev. 7:17).

> My Shepherd is the Lamb,
>   The living Lord, who died;
> With all that's truly good I am
>   Most plenteously supplied.
>
> He richly feeds my soul
>   With manna from above,
> And leads me where the rivers roll
>   Of everlasting love.
>
> My table he doth spread
>   With choicest fare, and I
> Behold the Lamb, the living Bread,
>   And eat most joyfully.
>
> He makes my cup run o'er,
>   Anointeth me with oil;
> I shall enjoy for evermore
>   The merits of his toil.

Then I my Shepherd's care
  Shall praise, and him adore,
And in his Father's house shall share
  True bliss for evermore.

I Am Jesus' Little Lamb
Henriette Louise von Hayn

1778

Henriette von Hayn taught in a Moravian girls' school and cared for the invalid sisters of the community. She died at Herrnhut in 1782. This beautiful hymn was translated from German.

> I am Jesus' little lamb,
>   Ever glad at heart I am;
> For my Shepherd gently guides me,
>   Knows my need, and well provides me.
> Loves me every day the same,
>   Even calls me by my name.
>
> Day by day, at home, away,
>   Jesus is my staff and stay.
> When I hunger, Jesus feeds me,
>   Into pleasant pastures leads me;
> When I thirst, he bids me go
>   Where the quiet waters flow.
>
> Who so happy as I am,
>   Even now the Shepherd's lamb?
> And when my short life is ended,
>   By his angel host attended,
> He shall fold me to his breast,
>   There in his arms to rest.

Awake My Soul
Samuel Medley

1782

Samuel Medley departed from the faith of his parents and grandparents until, convalescing from a serious injury, he was compelled to listen to his grandfather read to him a sermon by Isaac Watts that led to his conversion. Medley became a preacher in the Particular Baptist denomination and a hymn writer.

> Awake, my soul, in joyful lays,
>   And sing thy great Redeemer's praise;
> He justly claims a song from thee:
>   His lovingkindness, O how free!
>
> He saw me ruined in the Fall,
>   Yet loved me, not withstanding all;
> He saved me from my lost estate:
>   His lovingkindness, O how great!
>
> Though numerous hosts of mighty foes,
>   Though earth and hell my way oppose,
> He safely leads my soul along:
>   His lovingkindness, O how strong!
>
> Often I feel my sinful heart
>   Prone from my Saviour to depart;
> But though I have him oft forgot,
>   His lovingkindness changes not.

Soon shall I pass the gloomy vale,
　Soon all my mortal powers must fail;
O may my last expiring breath
　His lovingkindness sing in death!

Then let me mount and soar away
　To the bright world of endless day;
And sing with rapture and surprise
　His lovingkindness in the skies.

GRACIOUS SAVIOUR, GENTLE SHEPHERD
JANE LEESON[4]

1842

Gracious Saviour, gentle Shepherd,
   Our little ones are dear to thee;
Gathered with thine arms and carried
   In thy bosom may they be
Sweetly, gently, safely tended,
   From all want and danger free.

Tender Shepherd, never leave them,
   From thy fold to go astray;
By thy look of love directed,
   May they walk the narrow way;
Thus direct them, and protect them,
   Lest they fall an easy prey.

Let thy holy word instruct them;
   Fill their minds with heav'nly light;
Let thy love and grace constrain them
   To approve whate'er is right,
Take thine easy yoke and wear it,
   And to prove the burden light.

Cleanse their hearts from sinful folly
   In the stream thy love supplied;
Mingled streams of blood and water
   Flowing from thy wounded side:
And to heav'nly pastures lead them,
   Where thine own still waters glide.

[4] Adapted by John Keble (1857).

'In Heavenly Love Abiding'
Anna L. Waring

1850

Anna Waring was born in South Wales in 1820. Descriptions of the Christian life in her poetry are both strong and tender, brave and trustful.

In heavenly love abiding,
　No change my heart shall fear;
And safe is such confiding,
　For nothing changes here:
The storm may roar without me,
　My heart may low be laid;
But God is round about me,
　And can I be dismayed?

Wherever he may guide me,
　No want shall turn me back;
My Shepherd is beside me,
　And nothing shall I lack:
His wisdom ever waketh,
　His sight is never dim;
He knows the way he taketh,
　And I will walk with him.

Green pastures are before me,
　Which yet I have not seen;
Bright skies will soon be o'er me,
　Where the dark clouds have been:

My hope I cannot measure,
 My path to life is free;
My Saviour is my treasure,
 And he will walk with me.

The King Of Love My Shepherd Is
Henry W. Baker

1868

When Henry Baker died in 1877, he was comforted by the words of his version of Psalm 23.

> The King of love my Shepherd is,
>   Whose goodness faileth never;
> I nothing lack, if I am his,
>   And he is mine for ever.
>
> Where streams of living water flow,
>   My ransomed soul he leadeth,
> And, where the verdant pastures grow,
>   With food celestial feedeth.
>
> Perverse and foolish oft I strayed,
>   But yet in love he sought me,
> And on his shoulder gently laid,
>   And home rejoicing, brought me.
>
> In death's dark vale I fear no ill,
>   With thee, dear Lord, beside me;
> Thy rod and staff my comfort still,
>   Thy cross before to guide me.
>
> Thou spread'st a table in my sight;
>   Thine unction grace bestoweth;
> And, oh, what transport of delight
>   From thy pure chalice floweth.

And so though all the length of days
    Thy goodness faileth never:
Good Shepherd, may I sing thy praise
    Within thy house for ever!

In God's Green Pastures

Orien Johnson

1956

Orien Johnson studied and taught music at Wheaton College. Anne and I have sweet memories of the Jamaica Bible College students singing this song.

In God's green pastures feeding by his cool waters lie;
  Soft in the evening walk my Lord and I,
All the sheep of his pasture
  Fare so wondrously fine, his sheep am I.

> *Sisters*: Waters cool
> *Brothers*: In the valley
> *Sisters*: Pastures green
> *Brothers*: On the mountain
> *Sisters*: In the evening
> *Everyone*: Walk my Lord and I.

> *Sisters*: Dark the night
> *Brothers*: In the valley
> *Sisters*: Rough the way
> *Brothers*: On the mountain
> *Sisters*: Step by step
> *Brothers*: Step by step
> *Everyone*: My Lord and I.

Through the streets of the city in the darkness of the night,
  Far from the fold, he heard my lonely cry,
Now I sit at his table in the palace of light,
  His sheep am I!

GOD KEEPS ME AS A SHEPHERD
KEEPS HIS FLOCK

FREDERICK BUECKNER

1981

Frederick Bueckner's *Godric* is a semi-fictionalized life of the twelfth-century medieval St Godric of Finchale. One day Godric heard Eric, a hermit who lived near Durham in England, perched in a tree like a squirrel, singing the Psalms in Latin. 'But for me,' said Godric, 'he put them into speech I understood.'

God keeps me as a shepherd keeps his flock.
I want for nought.

I bleat with hunger, and he pastures me in meadows
    green.
I'm thirsty, and he leads me forth to water cool and
    deep and still.

He hoists me to my feet when I am weak.

Down goodly ways he guides me with his crook,
For he himself is good.

Yea, even when I lose my way in shadows dark as death,
I will not fear,
For he is ever close at hand with rod and staff to
    succour me.

GOD, MY SHEPHERD!
EUGENE PETERSON

2002

This version of Psalm 23 is from *The Message*, a translation of the Bible by Eugene Peterson, Presbyterian pastor and professor of Spiritual Theology at Regent College in Vancouver, British Columbia.

God, my shepherd! I don't need a thing.

You have bedded me down in lush meadows,
You find me quiet pools to drink from.

True to your word, you let me catch my breath
And send me in the right direction.

Even when the way goes through Death Valley,
I'm not afraid when you walk at my side.
Your trusty shepherd's crook makes me feel secure.

You serve me a six-course dinner right in front of my enemies.
You revive my drooping head; my cup brims with blessing.

Your beauty and love chase after me every day of my life.
I'm back home in the house of God for the rest of my life.

I AM Is My Shepherd
Bruce K. Waltke

2010

This translation of Psalm 23 by Bruce Waltke accompanies his book *The Psalms as Christian Worship*. He uses 'I AM' rather than LORD for the name of God.

I AM is my shepherd, I do not want.

In green pastures he allows me to rest;
    by choice watering places he leads me.

My vitality he restores;
    he leads me in paths of righteousness
    for his name's sake.

Even though I walk in a dark ravine,
    I do not fear evil, for you are with me;
    Your rod and your staff, they comfort me.

You prepare before me a table
    in the presence of my enemies;
    You anoint with oil my head;
    my cup overflows.

Surely goodness and kindness
    will pursue me all the days of my life,
    and I will return to dwell in the house of *I AM*
    for endless days.

WHA IS MY SHEPHERD

'SHEPHERD'S VERSION' OF PSALM 23 IN SCOTTISH DIALECT

I found these words on the wall of a croft in the Scottish Highlands. The source and date are unknown to me.

> Wha is my Shepherd, weel I ken,
>   The Lord himsel' is he;
> He leads me whaur the girse is green,
>   An' burnies quaet that be.
>
> Aft times I fain astray wad gang,
>   An' wann'r far awa';
> He finds me ott, he pits me richt,
>   An' brings me hame an' a'.
>
> Tho' I pass through the gruesome cleugh,
>   Fin' I ken he is near;
> His muckle crook will me defen',
>   Sae I hae nocht to fear.
>
> Ilk comfort whilk a sheep could need,
>   His thoctfu' care provides;
> Tho' wolves an' dogs may prowl aboot,
> In safety me he hides.
>
> His guidness an' his mercy baith,
>   Nae doot will bide wi' me;
> While faulded on the fields o' time,
>   Or o' eternity.

BIBLIOGRAPHY

Anders, Isabel, *Walking with the Shepherd* (Nashville: Nelson, 1994).

Often distant from the psalm's meaning, but with some helpful thoughts.

Bailey, Kenneth E., *The Good Shepherd: A Thousand Year Journey from Psalm 23 to the New Testament* (Downers Grove: IVP Academic, 2014).

The author writes, 'For nearly fifty years, Middle Eastern Shepherds with their flocks were a part of the larger context in which I grew up and then lived and taught the New Testament' (13). Bailey's book explores the many references to sheep and shepherds in the Bible.

Billings, J. Todd, *Rejoicing in Lament: Wrestling with Incurable Cancer & Life in Christ* (Grand Rapids: Brazos Press, 2015).

One of the best books about cancer and how to face it in a biblically faithful and theologically accurate way.

Bonhoeffer, Dietrich, *My Soul Finds Rest: Reflections on the Psalms* (Grand Rapids: Zondervan, 2002).

A collection of some of Bonhoeffer's sermons, thoughts, and poems on the Psalms. Often powerful and moving.

—*Psalms: The Prayer Book of the Bible* (Minneapolis: Augsburg, 1970).

Bonhoeffer classified the Psalms under the headings of the Creation, the Law, the Story of Salvation, the Messiah, the Church, Life, Suffering, Guilt, the Enemy, and the End.

Boreham, F. W., *In Pastures Green: A Ramble through the Twenty-third Psalm* (John Broadbanks Pub., 2011).

Boreham wrote: 'I discover with surprise that, although I have been preaching, after a fashion, for more than sixty years, I have never dealt with the Twenty-third Psalm. After conferring with other ministers of long experience, I have reached the conclusion that the omission is a fairly common one. We look wistfully at the Song of the Shepherd, but are afraid to tackle it.' His little book, Boreham wrote, 'was born of a profound personal experience.' His daughter, who had lived with her parents all her life, sickened and died. 'I fondly hope,' Boreham wrote that the book 'will pour into the hearts of its readers something of the comfort and grace that the Shepherd Psalm has, in my eighty-third year, ministered to me' (viii, 1).

Bunyan, John, *The Pilgrim's Progress* (Edinburgh: Banner of Truth Trust, 1977).

Calhoun, David B., *Knowing God and Ourselves: Reading Calvin's Institutes Devotionally* (Edinburgh: Banner of Truth Trust, 2017).

Calvin, John, tr. Robert White, *Sermons on the Beatitudes*, (Edinburgh: Banner of Truth Trust, 2006)

Chapman, J. Wilbur, *The Secret of a Happy Day: Quiet Hour Meditations* (Boston and Chicago: United Society of Christian Endeavour, 1899).

Thirty-one short meditations on Psalm 23.

Charry, Ellen T., *Psalms 1–50: Sighs and Songs of Israel* in *Brazos Theological Commentary* (Grand Rapids: Brazos, 2015).

An academic commentary by a Princeton Seminary professor. She treats the Psalms with respect and avoids the extremes of Higher Criticism.

Cook, Faith, *Our Hymn Writers and Their Hymns* (Darlington: EP Books, 2015).

Survey of the lives of the greatest British hymn writers and discussion of their major contributions.

Dawson, Jane, *John Knox* (London: Yale, 2017).

Dunlop, John, *Finishing Well to the Glory of God: Strategies from a Christian Physician* (Wheaton: Crossway, 2011).

Excellent book exploring end of life issues. There are nine 'strategies': 1. Live Well. 2. Let Go Graciously. 3. Treasure God's Love; Love Him in Return. 4. Grow through Adversity. 5. Embrace a Biblical View of Life and Death. 6. Complete Your Agenda. 7. Make Appropriate Use of Technology. 8. Changing Gears from Cure to Comfort Care. 9. Rest in Jesus.

Durham, James, *Lectures on the Book of Job* (1759; repr. Grand Rapids: Reformation Heritage Books, 2003).

Eswine, Zack, *Spurgeon's Sorrows* (Fear, Ross-shire: Christian Focus, 2015).

Goldingay, John, *Psalms for Everyone, Part 1: Psalms 1-72*, (Philadelphia: Westmister John Knox Press, 2014)

Haboush, Stephen A., *My Shepherd Life in Galilee with the Exegesis of the Twenty-third Psalm* (New York: Harper and Brothers, 1927; reprinted by the author, 1949).
  Interesting stories from a thoughtful shepherd.

Havner, Vance, *Though I Walk Through the Valley* (New York: Revell, 1974).
  A 'testimony born of adversity' of the beloved Southern Baptist preacher, when his wife, Sara, was stricken with a debilitating and fatal disease.

Hengstenberg, Ernst Wilhelm, *Commentary on the Psalms*, volume 1 (Eugene: Wipf & Stock, 2005).
  Scholarly treatment of the Psalms (first published in 1842–1845) with careful attention to Hebrew words – and some to Luther's writings about the Psalms.

Henry, Matthew, *Matthew Henry's Commentary*, volume 3 (Peabody: Hendrickson, 1991).
  In his own inimitable fashion, Matthew Henry provides (as the subtitle states) 'the sense [of the passage] given, and largely illustrated with practical remarks and observations.'

Holladay, William L., *The Psalms through Three Thousand Years: Prayerbook of a Cloud of Witnesses* (Minneapolis: Fortress Press, 1995).

Keller, Timothy, *Walking with God through Pain and Suffering* (New York: Riverhead, 2013).

A valuable book combining theological insights and pastoral care. A book for careful study and spiritual help.

Keller, W. Philip, *A Shepherd Looks at Psalm 23* (Grand Rapids: Zondervan, 1970).

Some interesting insights from a man, who cared for sheep in Africa and Canada, but he goes too far in trying to derive spiritual truths from the habits of sheep and the practices of shepherds.

Kidner, Derek, *Psalms 1–72* and *Psalms 73–150* (Downers Grove: InterVarsity, 1973).

An outstanding work, combining careful scholarship with devotional application.

Kirkpatrick, A. F., *The Book of Psalms* (1902, reprinted by Grand Rapids: Baker, 1982).

Brief notes that are careful and pertinent.

Krikorian, Meshach Paul, *The Spirit of the Shepherd: An Interpretation of the Psalm Immortal* (Philadelphia: Krikorian, 1950).

Krikorian grew up in the late nineteenth century in the mountains near the city of Tarsus. He became a pastor, survived the Armenian genocide, and emigrated to the West. The book is dedicated 'to the memory of my beloved father who gave me the opportunity to become a shepherd and to the glory of the Great Shepherd whom it seeks to exalt.'

Kreeft, Peter, 'Shared Hells,' *Bread and Wine: Readings for Lent and Easter* (New York: Orbis, 2005).

Kuyper, Abraham, *To Be Near Unto God*. tr. John Hendrik de Vries (Grand Rapids: Baker Book House, 1979)

Lamsa, George M., *The Shepherd of All: The Twenty-third Psalm* (CreateSpace Independent Publishing Platform, 2014).

George Lamsa became a deacon of the Syrian Orthodox Church and translated the fourth-century Syriac Bible into English. He wrote in the Foreword of his book: 'My ancestors for untold generations were sheep-raising people. My father and my mother loved and tended sheep. I was raised in a sheep camp. We lived in a tent made of the hair of goats just as Abraham and Isaac did. Like other boys, I was taught and disciplined by the shepherd. Since my father was chief shepherd, I was taught through his wisdom.'

L'Engle, Madeleine, *Two Part Invention: The Story of a Marriage*, (Crosswick Journal) (New York: Farrar Straus & Giroux, 1988).

Lewis, C. S., *Reflections on the Psalms* (London: Geoffrey P. Bles, 1958).

An enlightening look at themes in the Psalms. Despite his mild Higher Criticism and deficient view of Scripture, to most of what Lewis writes an evangelical can say 'Amen.'

— *Letters to an American Lady* (Grand Rapids: Eerdmans, 1967).

— *The Problem of Pain* (New York: Macmillan Publishing Company, 1962).

— *They Stand Together: The Letters of C. S. Lewis to Arthur Greeves* (1914–1963), ed. Walter Hooper (London: Collins, 1979).

Lupton, Lewis, *A History of the Geneva Bible* (London: Fauconberg/Olive Tree, 1966-81), Volume 3.

Luther, Martin, *Luther's Works,* Volume 12 (St Louis: Concordia, 1955).
    Psalm 23 was 'expounded one evening [in 1536] after grace at the dinner table by Dr Martin Luther.'

MacDuff, John R., *The Shepherd and His Flock; or, The Keeper of Israel and the Sheep of His Pasture* (New York: Robert Carter and Brothers, 1866).
    Chapters on biblical references to sheep and shepherds. Some helpful ideas but discursive and confusingly organized.

MacMillan, J. Douglas, *The Lord our Shepherd* (Bryntirion: Evangelical Press of Wales, 1983)
    Sermons on Psalm 23 by a minister who in his youth worked twelve years as a shepherd on the hills of North Argyllshire, Scotland. Many interesting stories of sheep and shepherds.

MacLaren, Alexander, *The Psalms* (London: Hodder & Stoughton, 1892).
    Helpful thoughts from a British Baptist pastor.

Meyer, F. B., *The Shepherd Psalm* (New York: Revell, 1895).

Dedicated by the author to 'D. L. Moody, with love and thankfulness for the inspiration of his life and words, from the far-away days of my first pastorate at York, to weeks of happy fellowship in Northfield Conventions.'

— *Daily Prayers* (Fearn, Ross-shire: Christian Focus, 2007).

This book of short prayers for every day in the year has helped and blessed me throughout my life. See my 'Sketch of the Life of F. B. Meyer' and 'My Daily Prayer' in the introduction.

Miller, Patrick D., *Interpreting the Psalms* (Philadelphia: Fortress, 1986).

The Professor of Old Testament Theology at Princeton Seminary writes about the Psalms and includes an exposition of ten selected psalms, including Psalm 23.

— *The Lord of the Psalms* (Philadelphia: Westminster/John Knox, 2013).

Chapters largely adapted from Miller's *Stone Lectures* at Princeton Seminary in 2010.

Monod, Adolphe, *Christian Suffering* (Amazon Kindle, 2017).

Monod's Farewell in a new translation by Campbell Markham. Monod gave his farewell sermons to a group of friends who gathered around his bed on Sunday afternoons to celebrate the Lord's Supper. His 'farewell' displays the heroism of Christian suffering.

Morgan, F. Crossley, *A Psalm of an Old Shepherd: A*

Devotional Study of Psalm 23 (London: Marshall, Morgan & Scott).

The son of G. Campbell Morgan views Psalm 23 as the memories of David about the way the Lord had led and cared for him.

Morgan, G. Campbell, *Notes on the Psalms* (New York: Revell, 1947).

Dedicated to David Martyn Lloyd-Jones: 'My valued and beloved colleague the last years of my active ministry; a man loyal to the word, and a preacher of exceptional ability.'

Motyer J. A., *New Bible Commentary, 21st Century Edition* (Grand Rapids: Eerdmans, 1970).

Brief, helpful comments on Psalm 23.

Norris, Kathleen, *Acedia & Me: A Marriage, Monks, and a Writer's Life* (New York: Riverhead Books, 2008),

O'Connor, Flannery, *Letters of Flannery O'Connor: The Habit of Being* (New York: Farrar, Straus and Giroux, 1979).

Palmer, Benjamin M., *The Life of James Henley Thornwell* (1875; repr. Edinburgh: Banner of Truth Trust, 1975)

Parkening, Christopher, *Grace Like a River* (Carol Stream, IL: Tyndale House, 2006).

Perowne, Stewart, *The Book of Psalms*, Volume 1 (Grand Rapids: Zondervan, 1966).

C. H. Spurgeon wrote that Perowne's work, first

published in 1864, 'is a masterpiece of extraordinary learning and critical skill' (*Commenting and Commentaries*, 89).

Plumer, William S., *Psalms: A Critical and Expository Commentary with Doctrinal and Practical Remarks* (Edinburgh: Banner of Truth Trust, 1975)

Plumer's massive commentary on the Psalms is, in my opinion, one of the best.

Prothero, Roland E., *The Psalms in Human Life* (London: Thomas Nelson, 1903)

A rich collection of notes and stories on how the psalms have been used by Christians throughout history.

Robinson, Haddon W., *Trusting the Shepherd: Insights from Psalm 23* (Carnforth, Lancashire: Discovery House, 2002)

Insights from a notable preacher.

Rutledge, Fleming, *Help my Unbelief* (Grand Rapids: Eerdmans, 2000)

— *The Undoing of Death* (Grand Rapids: Eerdmans, 2005)

Ryle, J. C., *The Power and Sympathy of Christ* (Edinburgh: Banner of Truth Trust, 2018).

Studies on John 11 (the death and raising of Lazarus) drawn from his *Expository Thoughts on the Gospel of John*, in which the author discusses such great subjects as sorrow, sickness, death, the grave, and, above all, the power and sympathy of Christ.

Selderhuis, Herman J., ed., *Reformation Commentary on Scripture*, Volume 7: *Psalms 1–72*, (Downers Grove: Inter-Varsity, 2015).

Extracts from the writings of Luther, Calvin, and other Reformation figures.

Spurgeon C. H., *The Treasury of David*, third edition (New York: Funk & Wagnalls, 1885).

Famous multi-volume work on the Psalms containing an exposition of each psalm, a collection of relevant quotations from other writers and 'homiletical hints to the village preacher.'

— *New Park Street Pulpit* and *Metropolitan Tabernacle Pulpit* (Pasadena, TX: Pilgrim Publications, 1971).

— *The Cheque Book of the Bank of Faith* (Fearn, Ross-shire,: Christian Focus, 1996)

Tallach, Fraser, *Fraser: Not a Private Matter* (Edinburgh: Banner of Truth Trust, 2003)

A human story of grace and suffering.

Thomson, W. M., *The Land and the Book or Biblical Illustrations drawn from the Manners and Customs, the Scenes and Scenery of the Holy Land* (London: Thomas Nelson, 1894).

William Thomson spent thirty years as a missionary in Syria and Palestine. In 1857 he and a friend made a pilgrimage 'from Dan to Beersheba.' Thomson published an account of their travels and experiences in *The Land and the Book*.

VanGemeren Willem, *The Expositor's Bible Commentary* (Grand Rapids: Zondervan, 1991), Volume 5, 214-19
    Treatment of Psalm 23 by an evangelical scholar.

Waltke, Bruce K. & Houston, James M., *The Psalms as Christian Worship: A Historical Commentary* (Grand Rapids: Eerdmans, 2010)
    Impressive scholarship from two respected writers. They provide in-depth commentary on thirteen psalms, including Psalm 23.

Weiser, Artur, *The Psalms* (Philadelphia: Westminster Press, 1962)
    Solid, devout scholarship.

BOOKS BY THE SAME AUTHOR
PUBLISHED BY THE TRUST

Swift and Beautiful, the Amazing Stories of Faithful Missionaries, paperback, 240 pp.

In Their Own Words, the Testimonies of Luther, Calvin, Knox, and Bunyan, paperback, 240 pp.

Knowing God and Ourselves, Reading Calvin's Institutes Devotionally, cloth-bound, 360 pp.

Our Southern Zion, Old Columbia Seminary (1828–1927), cloth-bound, 408 pp.

Pleading for a Reformation Vision, the Life and Selected Writings of William Childs Robinson, cloth-bound, 336 pp.

Prayers on the Psalms, from the Scottish Psalter of 1595, paperback, 152 pp.

Princeton Seminary, Volume 1: Faith & Learning, 1812–1868, cloth-bound, 528 pp.

Princeton Seminary, Volume 2: The Majestic Testimony, 1869–1929, cloth-bound, 592 pp.